THE GLASS DESK

GET YOUR FREE GIFT!

This book is all about self-reflection. You will be asking the Lord, and yourself, a lot of questions, so we created a cute guided journal just for you! It's the perfect place to record your prayers, thoughts, and revelations during this journey.

To download your copy, visit:
www.glassdeskbook.com

THE GLASS DESK

FROM DEFEATED TO REDEEMED
HEAL FROM YOUR PAIN
AS YOU CLEAN UP YOUR PAST AND UNFOLD YOUR FUTURE

AJ WILT

GLASS DESK PUBLISHING

Glass Desk Publishing | PO Box 92547 | Southlake, TX 76092

LCCN: 2020940536
ISBN: 978-1-7350194-0-6 (hardcover) | ISBN: 978-1-7350194-1-3 (paperback)
ISBN: 978-1-7350194-2-0 (ebook) | ISBN: 978-1-7350194-3-7 (audio book)

This book is dedicated to the Three in One, God of the Universe—Father, Son, and Holy Spirit—with the prayer that it will be received as a first fruits offering and be used to bless and encourage many of His children.

CONTENTS

INTRODUCTION

The Glass Desk. Not only is the desk glass, but it is mirrored. A place of reflection. A place full of light and life. I explain how the glass desk came to be in one of the following chapters, but first, I want to encourage you to take a seat at your glass desk. I want you to take a good hard look into that mirror until you see nothing but the redemption of Christ staring you back in the face.

As Christians, we often profess that our identity lies only in Christ. However, when looking into a mirror, the last thing we find ourselves thinking about is our fullness in Christ. All we see are the smudges left on the glass by others—their marks distorting our image.

Have you written all over your mirror with lipstick or dry erase markers as you try to hide behind a facade? Is your mirror cracked, or worse yet, broken with missing pieces—leaving you with jagged, sharp edges that you are afraid to touch? Is your mirror too small, and you are feeling constrained by your circumstances?

Maybe your mirror has a deep haze that no exterior cleaner can reach, and you feel a bit hopeless that it will ever be made clean. Has your mirror lost its ability to reflect light? Has the loss of light allowed a sense of darkness to linger—darkness that keeps your reflection from shining as radiantly as it should?

What do you think would happen if we sought out the One who could clean our mirrors and wipe away all the smudges? A Master Craftsman who could smooth those sharp edges? He would seal the cracks and has a cleaner strong enough to remove the haze embedded deep within your glass. He can fix our mirrors. He can shift our circumstances, and He will provide a mirror large enough for your entire reflection.

I know this Craftsman. His name is Jesus. When we call upon Jesus to fix our mirrors, we no longer have to dwell with a sense of darkness. His mirror reflects the perfect amount of light, and it casts out all darkness.

We all love hearing analogies that relate to our struggles and experiences. It's encouraging knowing that somebody else has that same deep haze lingering in their mirror. We find comfort knowing we aren't the only ones with issues.

As encouraging as it might be to know we are not alone in our struggles, we still need to seek the One who can fix our mirror. Jesus died so that we would have life abundantly. He doesn't want us dwelling with a dirty, broken mirror. He wants our mirror to reflect His perfect light.

Many Christians invite the Lord into their home and are happy to show Him around. However, as soon as He sees their mirror, and reaches out to fix it, they grab His hand to make Him stop. They are afraid He might cut His hand on the broken glass.

They worry the chemicals needed for deep cleaning are too dangerous. They politely thank Jesus for coming to their home but insist they will fix the mirror later, on their own time. They usher the Lord back to their beautiful living room and leave Him there while they go work on their reflection. We think to ourselves, *The Lord has our heart, and that's all that matters, right? We don't want to burden Him with something we can take care of on our own.*

From new believers to elders, this mistake is made again and again—sometimes without our even realizing it has happened. The simple fingerprints left by others begin to distort our image.

We don't bother the Lord with it because it's only a little smudge. We have a glass cleaner to wipe it up in a jiffy!

Unfortunately, each person has ten fingers, and we only have one rag to try and wipe it all clean. Our exposure to people and situations will overwhelm our little cleaning rag. We will tire of trying to keep it clean ourselves and will lose ground in the battle for our image, our identity, and our reflection.

How can I speak all of this with such confidence? I've walked it. Without realizing it, I had taken the cleaning rag from the Lord and was trying to keep the fingerprints at bay on my own. I didn't know they weren't ordinary prints. Those fingers had corrosive acid on them. What I thought was a normal smudge, wasn't. It had eaten through part of my reflection and left a wound. Wounds that were unknowingly attacking my heart. With the goal to distort the truth of the Father's love.

We need to be willing to take a good hard look at why our mirror cracked, determine whose smudges are scattered about, and be ready to let the Lord into those areas of our lives. Allowing Jesus to do the cleaning is how we shift from having a dirty mirror to one that reflects His redemption.

This book is a very personal journey. It was born out of pure heartache and the realization that too many smudges had dirtied up my mirror. There are many questions ahead, and some of them can be uncomfortable. If we are willing to take an honest look and surrender, Jesus is always faithful to answer and heal.

My image, identity, and reflection needed to be freshly redeemed. The truth of Jesus' redemption needed, once again, to make the journey from my mind to my heart.

It's time to take a seat at your glass desk. Your desk of redemption awaits. On the other side of this journey are newness, freedom, and healing—a new level of transparent intimacy with the Lord that will bring light back to your darkest places. I know— I walked the path and saw the goodness it brings. My route took much longer to walk as the Lord did His work, and I know He intends to use my journey to quicken yours. It's time to jump into His refreshing waters and spring up with new life!

Transparency illuminates excellent testimonies of the Lord's love and redemption. I'm placing myself on display as I walk you through various parts of my story, and I am asking you to do the same. Put it all out there for the Lord to see. Ask Him the hard questions and dig until He plucks every bitter root from your innermost being. Don't leave even one stone unturned. There might be tears, but there will be a revelation. Don't shy away from this opportunity.

However, if transparency is of little value in your eyes and you are not willing to go beyond the surface, then this book is probably not for you. If you want a book that is all happy rainbows and has the answers to all life's questions, then I can't help you. I don't have all the answers. I have one answer: ask Jesus. He is faithful to answer. Use this book as a prompting. Use it as an excuse to dig deeper and deal with issues that have been lingering on the back burner.

The italicized paragraphs below were the start of this book. It all poured out of me one sad, lonely, winter evening while sitting in my bed with my laptop and a tissue box. The outside chill, coupled with the recent coldness from my loved one, sent a chill so deep into my being that I shivered and shook as I typed the words.

Tears poured from my swollen, red eyes and streamed down my quivering cheeks where they splattered on my keyboard. As I peered through my tear-stained glasses, I had a lot of pain and questions that I needed to ask the Father. I was distraught with sadness and could do nothing other than press into His faithfulness. It was one of those traumatic life moments that seemed to etch itself into my memory bank. It was a life-changing night as I typed and typed.

I sit here in heartache. The deep heartache that can only be understood by those who have experienced its hollow, suffocating emptiness. A hope, recently, realized as lost. Relationships reaching a new level of fracture. A chasm so deep and wide that to ponder crossing seems beyond fanciful.

I have concluded that life is both the greatest struggle and most joyous experience we will ever entertain. Maybe you understand that statement. Perhaps you do not. Character is built during times of struggle and pain. Times of trial mold us into our greatest selves. As we walk through this human experience, each of us has a path unique to our strengths, weaknesses, triumphs, and failures.

Is heartache finally to be the catalyst for my writing? Will heartache be the catalyst for you to start that company, make that phone call, or finally commit to the lifestyle changes you have never felt motivated to begin? Will your heartache finally lead you to the foot of the cross so that Jesus can redeem all your tears?

Why is heartache such a powerful motivator? Why have so many hit songs been borne out of pure sorrow and pain? What is it that takes us from crushing pain to crushing triumph? How do we navigate the waters that exist between our distress and promises of hope and joy?

How do we emerge from beneath the rock of defeat so we can stand atop that rock with our banner of redemption boldly waving? How do we finish the journey to our promised land victoriously?

I hope you are not in a valley at this current moment in life. I hope your wilderness season has ended, and you are currently high atop a mountain. I still ask that you walk this journey. Let there be healing where you didn't realize you needed it. Open your eyes to see the fullness of God's Redemption. Let the Holy Spirit remove all blinders from past hurts so nothing is hindering your view of Christ's redemption.

I urge you to join me as I dive into my past, my present, and my future. I hope that through sharing my unique path, you will see the value in yours. I want you to join me as I ask myself the hard questions. I hope that you will learn to appreciate your sufferings, your bliss, and the events contributing to those opposing realities. Dive feet first with the Lord into your past, present, and future. The waters may feel deep and seem rough at times, but we can do this together. Jesus can silence any storm. It's time for healing, redemption, and a new beginning!

CHAPTER 1

DETOUR

HOW TO HANDLE THE PAIN

I planned to tell you how to embrace your pain. We were going to discuss how the trials we face are a way for us to become more like Christ. I planned to help you understand James 1:2-4 NLT: "Dear brothers and sisters, when troubles of any kind come your way, consider it an opportunity for great joy. For you know that when your faith is tested, your endurance has a chance to grow. So let it grow, for when your endurance is fully developed, you will be perfect and complete, needing nothing."

We were going to learn the proper way to give a big bear hug to all those trials, and we were going to like it.

Nope. Detour.

So, I have this amazing friend. We know each other because we were both employed at a local university many years ago. We do our best to stay in touch via email and try to find time to visit every so often. I treasure our friendship because we always have the best fellowship, and she has one of those gentle souls—love pours out into those around her. You know the kind of person I am talking about—the one with eyes so bright the love of the Lord penetrates your soul; she is one of those people!

One day I received an email from her with the subject line: QUESTION. Yes, in all capital letters. In her email, she was asking my opinion about a message preached by my pastor. She was troubled by what seemed, at the time, to be a message implying our tests and trials are from God. This threw her caution flags high into the air, and she reached out to me to see if she and I were on the same page.

Her stance was that our Father God does not test us. She was not talking about the happenings He allows as a regular part of our human existence in a fallen world but was referring to the fact that suffering and trials are not *sent* to us by His hands. She explained herself wonderfully. I agreed with and understood each part of her contention.

However, my mind became stuck on analytically looking at the base question. *Does God test us?* For the remainder of the day, that question would not leave my mind. I marveled at the mental real estate it was occupying. I knew there must be a reason the Lord allowed this innocent question to stay firmly lodged in my mind. I was intrigued! It was such a simple question to answer, and I already *knew* the answer. Therefore, I did what any average person, who knows the answer to a question, would do. I tossed any preconceived ideas out the window.

I was reading the book of Judges and recently read chapter two, so it was fresh on my mind. Judges 2:21-23 NLT, "I will no longer drive out the nations that Joshua left unconquered when he died. I did this to test Israel—to see whether or not they would follow the ways of the Lord as their ancestors did." That is why the Lord left those nations in place. He did not quickly drive them out or allow Joshua to conquer them all.

Right there! God Himself says, "I did this to test Israel." I wanted a simple objective way to answer her question, and the Lord provided. Right? I explained my logic and cited various supporting scriptures, concluding, yes, God can test us. My decision premised on the idea that testing, in and of itself, was not evil. This could only lead me to the conclusion that God can and does test us.

To my amazement, she did not see my literal and straightforward interpretation as an acceptable conclusion. I thought I nailed it! She had a very loving and thought-provoking response and maintained her original conviction on the topic. Another day passed as I mulled over this simple question. I didn't feel this question was worth all the mental energy I was losing to its contemplation, and I share her exact convictions on the topic.

Her responses were precisely in line with the teachings I follow as truth concerning our Heavenly Father and the topic of testing. You might be wondering, *Why did she seek a different answer than what she already knew to be the truth*? Great question!

My motivation for not agreeing and moving on was because of the mental energy the question had stolen. I knew if this simple question had been plaguing me for days, there must be something the Lord wanted me to uncover. He had a truth that needed to come to light. Was He trying to reveal we were wrong in our theologies? Was the Lord using this as a way for us to understand we needed to adjust our thinking?

I woke up on the third day of this discussion and immediately looked to see if I had an email. I did! Certainly, she was going to share fresh revelation!

She had no fresh revelation.

She had more explanations, already supporting what I knew to be true. I immediately thought, *God, what am I missing? Let me come to an understanding.* If we were not going to come across new revelation, then there was no point in all this effort. Why would He send me down this rabbit hole? When I reached a point of mild frustration, He reminded me of a previous email. My friend had mentioned something along the lines of, "Are you asking the right questions?"

With the Judges scripture still fresh on my mind, God had me rethink the nature of His test in that scripture. He showed me how what He left was a choice. If He had not left the other nations among the Israelites, then, by default, the Israelites would have worshiped Him.

There are choices for us to make every moment of every day, opportunities for us to exercise our free will. Tests, if you will. However, test, as it related to our conversation, should have been defined as punishment, or an arduous trial to cause suffering. I was relieved to have finally quantified "test."

Christ Jesus took the ultimate test, suffered the ultimate punishment, and made the ultimate sacrifice. He did it once, and He did it for all. As followers of Christ, we have all been eternally forgiven and have nothing to prove to our Father. The words I would use to address the question, "Does God punish (test) us?" would be, "A just God cannot accept Jesus' work on the cross as finished, then turn around and punish us." All our sins are forgiven because of our faith in the finished work of Jesus on the cross.

Going through all this finally led to me asking the right question. Given what I already knew to be accurate, why would I have taken the time to reconsider if God could test us? Why was I seemingly OK with being tested by God using both definitions?

My instinct was to prove testing was not evil; even though I knew the heart behind her question was related more to testing as a punishment. I never mentioned it in any of our emails, but I had decided it was merely because of my personality. My personality doesn't have a problem with being tested because I know God will always get me through it, and I will learn something from it. I will become more Christ-like in the process, and all will be well.

I continued to probe in this area and remembered how often I used to feel as if a trial *should* come when things seemed to be going well. It bothered me that my mind frequently defaulted to that thought. I concluded that I felt that way because I had already been through so many traumas in my life. It was mentally easier to expect the worst and hope for the best. That way, as a defense mechanism, I wouldn't be caught off guard or surprised by trials. Instead, I could look forward to the fruit of the hardship rather than getting stuck on the pain.

If you find yourself nodding in agreement, please reconsider! This trail of thought is not biblical. Expecting the worst and hoping for the best is a way to accept living a life of defeat instead of a life of victory. You may put the Christian icing on top of it, but expecting the worst and hoping for the best is robbing you of the richness and joy of God's grace.

When we convince ourselves to think this way, we are at direct odds with the word of the Lord. Proverbs 10:22 NLT, "The blessing of the Lord makes a person rich, and He adds no sorrow to it." Our Father in heaven does not supply according to a limited storehouse of blessings. Nobody has to lose for you to gain. You do not have to play a tit-for-tat game where God decides He will only bless you if He can also curse you. That's not how the grace of God works.

When we became believers in Christ, we entered the heavenly economy. We need to understand that God supplies from His never-ending storehouses. God does not have to rob Peter to pay Paul! The thought that there is even a limit to the blessings the Lord can pour upon you is not biblical. When you carry this tit-for-tat mentality, you have placed yourself back under the Law. Without realizing it, you begin operating in a works-based mindset.

Grace and works cannot coexist. You must choose which one will reign in your life. Will you live under the Law and works, or will you live under the freedom of grace? Romans 11:6 NRSV: "But if it is by grace, it is no longer on the basis of works; otherwise grace would no longer be grace."

I felt as if the Holy Spirit was nudging me to keep digging. I was more than happy to teach the truth to others. My mind fully understood that God does not punish us, and the choices we have each day are not tests as the term relates to punishment. My brain knew the truth, but my heart had slipped out of alignment with that truth. I realized this had nothing to do with personality.

I was trying to justify reserving some of God's wrath for myself. I was somehow allowing the finished work of the cross to be enough for others but felt it was OK if I still had to endure some wrath for my sins. I had placed myself back under the Law even though my lips spoke only of grace. It was a heart problem, and I needed the Lord to show me the root.

These were some profound revelations, and I had to remind myself that what was true for one child of God was true for them all. It led me to ask the Father what the root of my mindset was. *Why did I feel some wrath was OK for me? How had I slipped back into a works-based mentality and allowed the truth of His grace to escape my heart? Why had I allowed myself to accept living a life of defeat over a life of victory?*

The Lord responded, "Pride."

OK, not what I was expecting.

What I first thought was a defense mechanism against the pain of trials was not at all what it seemed. He showed me that by thinking I still deserved His wrath, I was saying Jesus' blood was good enough to cover everyone else's sin but was not good enough to cover my sin.

My heart sank.

The defense mechanism of expecting the worst, hoping for the best, while feeling I deserved some of God's wrath, was rooted in pride. Oh no! But how did that happen?

As I continued to dig deeper into prayer, the Holy Spirit showed me I had fresh wounds of rejection and abandonment. Those wounds, in short order, took me down a path of independence. If I were completely independent, then I would not need anybody. If you do not need anybody, then you won't be hurt when they abandon or reject you.

I had allowed an independent spirit to take root in my heart, and I became prideful in my independence. The spirit of independence was able to infiltrate my relationship with the Father. It worked quickly to remove the revelation of grace from my heart. I was none the wiser that it had happened because I still had head knowledge of His grace.

Grace and an independent spirit cannot coexist with one another because grace is all about our dependence upon Jesus' blood. If we are not continually leaning on God's grace, through Jesus, then we will find ourselves looking inward to our strength and reasoning. By default, when our solutions fail, we will accept that we deserve punishment for our shortcomings.

I had gone through healing for rejection and abandonment many years before, but with the new trials I had recently faced, I allowed them to retake root. The independent spirit kicked the truth of God's grace right out of my heart. The wounds of rejection and abandonment conjured up feelings of not being good enough for people to love, resulting in the thought that punishment for those shortcomings was acceptable.

I knew about the spirit of rejection and abandonment. However, I could never understand why I felt I deserved my trials or that something bad was around the corner. Pride developed a fleshly defense against those spiritual wounds. Allowing offense to take root in your heart will lead your flesh to create defense mechanisms rooted in fear.

I had unknowingly sacrificed the truth of His grace on the altar of fear and pride.

The disconnect between my mind and my heart had me deceived! I asked the Lord to soften my heart and remove the wall I had built. I again sought healing for the wounds of rejection and abandonment. I began focusing on the truth that my trials are not punishments for my sins. I had to speak to my heart and remind myself that I do not deserve any of the trials I face.

I am a child of God, and Jesus has already taken my trials and pain. The wounds of rejection and abandonment will distort our interpretation of the Father. We begin to search within ourselves for a solution to our pain so we won't hurt again, but in doing so, we allow our hearts to become hardened. Remember, grace needs a soft heart to take root and bear fruit.

GRACE AND MERCY

Let's talk about grace and mercy. Hebrews 4:16 ESV: "Let us then with confidence draw near to the throne of grace, that we may receive mercy and find grace to help in time of need." We often use the terms interchangeably, but it is important to differentiate the two. Mercy is when we are spared the punishment we should receive. Grace is the unmerited favor of God that gives us good things we don't deserve.

Imagine a person broke into your vehicle to steal your laptop. You could choose to show them mercy by not pressing charges. They won't receive the punishment they deserve because you have spared them. Showing them grace would mean not only did you show them mercy and not press charges, but you went ahead and gave them your laptop in their time of need.

Rejoice that our God is full of mercy and grace! The blood of Jesus keeps us from receiving punishment and simultaneously showers us with blessings. Romans 9:15-16 NLT: "For God said to Moses, 'I will show mercy to anyone I choose, and I will show compassion to anyone I choose.'" So it is God who decides to show mercy. We can neither choose it nor work for it.

Along the same lines, don't turn choosing grace into a new law. We were not created to choose grace but to receive grace. It is a gift freely given, not a gift we have to purchase with our works.

When we say that we are *choosing* grace, we immediately take the focus off Jesus and place it on ourselves. It's a way of saying to those around you, "Look at me! I chose grace. What have you done?" It creates a way to pour condemnation upon those who haven't done the work of choosing grace. It's a mentality rooted in pride, works, and the Law.

Grace suddenly becomes about your action, your choice, instead of being about Jesus' blood. Ephesians 2:8-9 ESV: "For by grace you have been saved through faith. And this is not your own doing; it is the gift of God, not a result of works, so that no one may boast."

If you ever find yourself boasting in your decision to choose grace, then you need to evaluate how the spirit of pride, works, or Law took root. By the direction of the Holy Spirit, quickly dig it out. James 4:6 NLT: "And he gives grace generously. As the Scriptures say, 'God opposes the proud but gives grace to the humble.'"

The fullness of the revelation of God's grace is a personal and unique walk for each believer. You can do nothing to expedite the revelation of God's grace. Worship, prayer, and revelation direct from the Holy Spirit are the only paths to more profound revelation. Deciding to *choose* grace is not going to bring you to revelation quicker. It will do the opposite and blind you once again with the Law and works. 2 Peter 1:2 NLT: "May God give you more and more grace and peace as you grow in your knowledge of God and Jesus our Lord." That's it right there! Seek to grow in your understanding of God and Jesus, and He will give you more and more grace—more and more unmerited favor!

Grace was never meant to be confiscated by the Law and turned into a magnifying glass. Don't allow grace to be manipulated into a tool for examining the salvation of those around you. Each person is to work out their own salvation with fear and trembling (Philippians 2:12). When grace becomes a magnifying glass, we begin to think that we can search out all faults and perfect His grace. The truth is that you can't improve His grace or the outcome of His grace. Again, Romans 11:6 ESV reminds us, "But if it is by grace, it is no longer on the basis of works; otherwise grace would no longer be grace."

Grace is meant to be a mirror, not a magnifying glass. God's grace in your life should reflect His goodness and the unmerited favor He pours upon His children. You don't need to try and keep the mirror clean or shine it. It is an eternal reflection of His blood upon your life.

Indeed, grace is a reflection of the goodness of the Father. He gives it to us to wear in testimony of His goodness. Grace is our perfect worship garment!

Imagine it this way; you are covered head to toe in a garment crafted from the most beautifully reflective gemstones God has ever created. As you stand before Christ and sing His praise, His image reflects back to Him. Grace is that garment of worship and the never-ending, perfect light of His glory reflects from it for all eternity.

On the other hand, do you know what magnifying glasses do when light shines through them? They catch things on fire. We have the choice to wear a garment of worship crafted from reflective gemstones or a garment crafted of magnifying glasses. I don't know about you, but the magnifying glass outfit sounds hot and very dangerous. Let's go ahead and leave those magnifying glasses in the junk drawer so we can use them for something a little less intense.

We must be honest with ourselves when we ask why heartache is such a powerful motivator. Heartache is such a powerful motivator because ingrained in our souls is the desire for justice. We long to see justice prevail while we cling to the hope of redemption.

Created in the image of a just God, we desire atonement for the wrongs committed against us. Frequently, a genuine apology is enough to satisfy our desire for justice—a simple acknowledgment that we were wronged. The problem arises when we conflate the passion for justice with our desire to "show them"—taking our God-given desire for justice and twisting it with our flesh-based desire to prove our worth. It is a recipe the spirit of pride knows by heart.

If you find heartache has been a source of motivation, then ask yourself why. Were you seeking to create justice?

In my introduction, I attribute my recent devastation as the motivator for my writing. I use my writing as a release and a way to connect with God. Often, I express my desires and prayers more effectively in writing than in speech. This book is a very personal journey I walked with the Lord—my journey, motivated by pain, that ushered me to the foot of the cross in search of healing.

There are tough questions you need to address when looking at why pain has motivated you. Has the agony of your situation thrown you to the feet of Jesus with a willing spirit to obey, follow where He leads, and rest in His grace? Or are you seeking to prove something out of your own strength?

Were you motivated after a hard break-up to "get in shape"? Were you motivated after being laid off to go to school and get your degree? Or to become "indispensable"? The Lord will use every part of our story to His glory and for the good of those who love Him. However, does that mean the decision to "show them" is the best one to take?

When we experience heartache, our motivation should come from Christ and His blessed assurance. If we see that it is coming from within our determination, we need to tap the brakes and seek His face. It can be effortless to get stuck in the cyclical pattern of heartache, show them, independence, pride, works. This pattern will manifest if anything other than the cross governs your motivation. Your determination to prove your worthiness is a fast track toward having the truth of God's grace slip from your heart. Basing your worthiness on works that will "show them" is a stealthy trap the enemy loves to use.

The "show them" mentality can manifest in many situations; for example, say a loved one dies of heart disease. We can slip into an attitude of showing them, "I won't die of heart disease." We begin doing every work we know of to keep our heart healthy. We try to show the grave it can't take us. We are trying to add to what Christ already finished. Jesus defeated the grave. All you need to do is receive that gift. To think that by eating lettuce and running five miles a day, you will somehow overcome the grave is an exercise in futility. Please hear me. I speak these words as a nutrition consultant! I know the power of a proper diet, but more than that, I know the power of our mighty God.

When you are working to show the grave, you won't fall victim to it; you open the door to the spirit of pride. Your triumph against the grave no longer becomes about the work of the Holy Spirit, and the redemptive blood of Jesus. It becomes about your discipline and works.

A key characteristic of the "show them" mentality is that it will cause you to take actions that go against your character. Acting out of character, or making brash decisions, are always red flags that you could be walking into some less-than-ideal territory.

Another trap laid by the enemy's use of the "show them" mentality is not rooted in pride but rooted in bitterness and a hardened heart. Maybe you have a family member who wronged you, and immediately you turn to, "I'll show them if I ever do that again." Or a friend doesn't meet your expectations, and you immediately set hard new boundaries that won't allow open communication, strangling any room for deepening of the friendship.

The decision to "show them" robs everybody of the joy that grace brings because a wall takes shape around the heart. We want that wall to protect us from injury, but it will also keep love from entering. Walls keep anything from getting in or out, and we slip into a state of isolation. Isolation causes us to develop the inability to be transparent and open in relationships. Again, allowing the potential to welcome an independent spirit.

During times of isolation, when we are far from the flock and the Shepherd, we become an easy target for the Devil. We want to avoid building monuments and idols of offense around our hearts. We will begin to worship them as we strive to keep them erect. The wall built to keep everyone out will also keep Jesus out. In His absence, our worship is then directed toward our offenses. A more productive route to take is one of grace, patience, and trying to understand what happened. Being slow to take offense and quick to forgive is going to set the stage for the fastest recovery.

Hear me loud and clear: I am not promoting that you become a Christian doormat. Don't become the catch-all for everyone's dirt. But don't jump to wall building or retaliation either. It is essential to evaluate each situation after the tempers have dissipated. Evaluate your own heart immediately. Have you resurrected a little wall from the offense? Catch it before the mortar has time to dry and kick it down.

Identify your tendencies in this area. If you tend to use that mortar and trowel to build walls, decide to hand that mortar and trowel over to Jesus. He would rather use those tools for building steps that bring you closer to Him than for walls. Forgive, speak healing over your heart, and move forward in the situation with grace and peace.

Boundaries are a crucial part of our lives as Christians. Proverbs 4:23 NLT: "Guard your heart above all else, for it determines the course of your life." We are to guard our hearts above all else, but guard does not mean isolate. Is there a particular relative or friend with a pattern of offense toward you? Reevaluate how much time you spend with them. Reconciliation is a two-way road where each party has to meet in the middle. Forgive the offenses and communicate whose court holds the ball.

Forgiveness is always appropriate for the healing of your heart and the avoidance of bitterness. However, reconciliation can look very different in each relational situation because more than one party is involved. Discernment from the Holy Spirit is paramount in guiding the correct steps to take during healing and reconciliation.

RELEASE THE PAIN

What's my point? Why did I share all this? I share this because we do not need to embrace our pain. Would you hug a cactus? I hope not. If we adopt the mentality of embracing pain, we enter into very unhealthy habits. We end up harboring a thought life, as I had, that convinces us we deserve our pain.

Embracing your pain is akin to having an unhealed injury with which you learned to cope. You can function with the pain. Thus, you never sought professional help in repairing the injury. Now, you walk with a limp.

Embracing pain is like letting the neighborhood skunk into your house because he hangs out on your porch all the time. We will have suffering in this life, but to embrace something our Father never created for us is very dangerous.

By embracing my pain, I had unknowingly trapped myself in the sin of pride. I wanted to "show them" I was fine on my own. Unfortunately, when we embrace our pain, we allow our soul to meditate on, and dwell with, a spirit with which God never intended we share communion.

When we allow those walls of offense to resurrect around our hearts, we find that as the mortar dries, little cracks begin to form. Our worship becomes focused on fixing those cracks with fresh mortar. We try to keep our defenses built up. However, we need to be more focused on tearing our walls down than building them up. Instead of mortar and trowel being at the ready, we need to keep our sledgehammer and wheelbarrow close at hand. We don't want to be instinctual wall builders. We want to be at the ready to demolish offenses built around our hearts.

Instead of embracing your pain and spiritual bondage, kick that stench to the curb. It's time for Pepé to find a new porch. Take your pain to Jesus. Will it disappear suddenly? It's possible. Remember, we are still human, and our soul can feel the sting of pain long after we have forgiven.

Trust in Him. He is faithful to redeem and restore our hearts. He has already taken all our pain unto Himself on the cross. Don't hang onto it any longer. Stop nailing things to your cross. He already suffered on your behalf. Release the offenses and walk in the peace that only He can give!

We need to recognize that as God's children, our sins have been completely atoned for and forgiven. Sins from our past, sins from our present, and sins we have yet to commit are all forgiven if we will only choose to turn with repentant hearts back toward the cross. 1 Peter 3:18 AMP: "For indeed Christ died for sins once for all, the Just and Righteous for the unjust and unrighteous [the Innocent for the guilty] so that He might bring us to God, having been put to death in the flesh, but made alive in the Spirit." Christ was crucified nearly two thousand years ago, once, for all. None of us existed, yet atonement had been paid for our sins.

All sin is covered in the redemptive Blood of The Lamb for those who receive His gift of grace. Yes, we will face trials in this life, and God will use them to make us more Christ-like. Glory will come to the Father through the triumph of our trials. Yes, we will endure consequences for poor decisions. Life will not be a stroll in the park because we are Christians, but hear me loud and clear; you do not deserve your pain. Do not reserve God's wrath for yourself! Jesus has already taken all of it.

If you frequently expect the worst or feel you deserve your misfortunes and pain, then I am begging you to ask yourself why. Pray and dig deep. Find out why you are embracing the pain. For me, it was a spirit of rejection and abandonment. I became very independent as a defense measure to avoid being hurt and allowed it to morph into pride. I was extremely proud not to need anybody!

Maybe you are harboring unforgiveness against yourself. Perhaps you also have a spirit of rejection. Assess the root of your motivation. Evaluate if your motivation is a healthy, earnest quest for healing or if it's rooted in the "show them" mentality.

Only the Holy Spirit can guide you in this journey, and I implore you to seek Him out and ask these hard questions. John 14:26 AMP: "But the Helper (Comforter, Advocate, Intercessor—Counselor, Strengthener, Standby), the Holy Spirit, whom the Father will send in My name [in My place, to represent Me and act on My behalf], He will teach you all things. And He will help you remember everything I have told you."

Seek fresh revelation in pursuit of your freedom. Our Father is faithful to provide!

Primary Takeaways

- You do not deserve your pain—don't embrace it!
- Do not reserve God's wrath for yourself. Receive His grace!
- Do not glorify your pain by nailing it to your cross.
- Identify the root of your wrong belief and dig it out.
- Examine your motivation.

Action Steps/Journaling Topics

- Where is the disconnect between what your mind knows to be true and what you believe in your heart?
- Have you become comfortable with your pain? List the situations and ask yourself why.

- Are you walking with a limp in any area of your life? When did it develop, and why have you chosen not to address it?

- Do you feel you deserve your pain? Why?

- Are you reserving some of God's wrath for yourself? Why?

- What grudges are you holding against yourself or others?

- In what ways has heartache been a motivator in your life? Explain.

- Was the motivation based on Christ's direction for your life or in your pride?

- Ask a close friend for their observations and receive from them without ears of offense.

Chapter 2

From Defeat to Redemption

Logically Speaking

Defeated, hopeless, heartbroken; most of us have become well acquainted with these feelings at one point or another—a failed relationship, a wayward child, the loss of a loved one, a promotion missed. Sometimes we are completely blindsided by the unfortunate events in our lives. Other times we are more than aware of the coming tragedy.

I sit and ponder this idea after the passing of my beloved fourteen-year-old cat, Baby. Her health had been declining for the past few months, and I had ample time to adjust to her coming fate. However, when the tragedy struck, and she took her final breath, I wept so bitterly I cannot adequately explain the scene. The depth of the sorrow I felt within my being was an utterly nauseating sense of emptiness.

Why, if I knew what was coming, did it still cause such a crushing response? If her life had unexpectedly ended, would I be feeling any less heartbroken?

What the Father revealed to me is that I became defeated before the tragedy even happened. For months and months, I was in a desert place. I cried out to God, went through periods of frustration, and felt as if I was entirely disconnected. I slipped into a state of depression that left me feeling unmotivated, directionless, and overwhelmed. How is such a response possible before the occurrence of the actual tragedy? How do we become frozen before heartbreak even strikes?

We fail to recognize that the future tragedy is the root of our shifting demeanor, overwhelm, and defeat. How can it be possible for an event yet to happen to be the root of a problem? Doesn't the root have to be established first? I had begun to mourn an event that had yet to come. I am a child of God, but instead of focusing on His promises, I allowed myself to begin meditating on defeat, sadness, and loss. I was believing based on earthly vision instead of staying focused on the truths spoken by God.

LOGIC IS THE ENEMY OF FAITH

We become frozen before the heartbreak comes because we shift our focus from the spiritual to the physical. Instead of rejoicing in another day with our loved one, we begin to try and prepare ourselves for the inevitable. In doing so, we shift our focus from meditating on what is good, right, and holy, to meditating on what is earthly. Meditating on what is earthly will never lead to the inner peace that God has for us.

To get from pain to triumph, we must rid ourselves of earthly logic and reason. Living a triumphant life and navigating the rough waters between our hurt and our promised land is done void of human reasoning. We must forego earthly logic while simultaneously being thrust at the foot of the cross. We must stay focused on His promises no matter how our circumstances look.

We must exchange our earthly glasses for brand new spiritual ones! It's like taking off cheap sunglasses and putting on a brand-new pair of fancy fishing sunglasses. Everything around you looks completely different! No more distracting glares or washed-out colors. Instead, you have a clear view of the colorful scenery and the abundant catch awaiting you!

Logic and reason are two tools used to create a root in our minds for a problem that hasn't happened yet. Let's think *logically* for a minute. *You are too young for that promotion. Your best days are behind you, and you should retire. Your skill level is not adequate. You can't stop the inevitable. Your ideas are not very original. You could never afford that house.* Sound like anybody you know? Whoa, me too! We learn to be rational, reasonable, and logical by the standards of this world.

I am convinced that reason and logic are some of the enemy's favorite tools. Logic and reason shift your focus to earthly outcomes and standards. They are a tool used to shift your focus off the grace of God. What better way to take you from operating under the covenant of grace than to overwhelm you with logic?

Logic is the perfect high-speed railway to usher you back into operating under the Law. Logic and reason are the teeth of that roaring lion, the Devil. He tries to sink his canines deep into your leg and drag you straight back into a works-based mentality. The truth of God's grace gets ripped from our hearts when we allow the lies of logic and reasoning to take root. It's a stealthy attack that can leave us deceived.

You know the truth of God's grace in your mind, but logic and reason cannot cohabitate in your heart with God's grace. Your heart will meditate on logic and reason, or it will meditate on His unmerited favor. There isn't room for entertaining both.

Don't misunderstand me. Critical thinking and logic are a significant part of a healthy and productive life. If water and electricity do not mix, then it is best not to use your hairdryer in the tub. That is an excellent application of rational thinking. We have many precautionary measures we take that are merely good habits. We buckle our seat belts, we have insurance policies to protect our cars, homes, and loved ones. We don't handle poisonous animals or eat things not made for human consumption. We practice proper financial habits. These are all simple functions that allow us to live healthy, safe lives and minimize potential risks.

We get into trouble when we begin to apply logic and reason to the intangible parts of our lives. We make the mistake of meditating on all those hypothetical situations. The battle we wage is not against flesh and blood, but against principalities and powers in the spiritual realm (Ephesians 6:12). We should use critical thinking, but the spiritual realm does not operate in a way we can explain using the world's standards.

When we try to apply our earthly logic to spiritual matters, we start doing Satan's bidding for him. I can think of no worse idea than to begin applying logic and reason to your hopes and dreams! The deep desires of our hearts go beyond the physical. Frequently, those desires and passions are placed there by the Lord Himself. However, we refuse even to attempt to attain them because we focus on them being *impossible*. The pursuit of your dreams may not be leisurely, but they are never impossible when your focus is on the promises and will of God for your life.

How do we identify the intangibles? It may be easier to identify the tangibles first. The tangibles engage our senses or operate in our lives in a "matter-of-fact" way. Using logic to assess the outcomes of the tangibles bears consistent results, or results in a general practice of safety. The intangibles are everything else!

The intangibles are one of the greatest gifts given to us by our Father. The intangibles live deep in the psyche. They allow us to ponder the creation around us, contemplate the purpose of life, and experience love and hope. The intangibles are all the possibilities and variables in our lives. If our lives only consisted of tangibles, there would be no reason for faith.

There is no worse existence than to require proof or an explanation for everything. If you continually need an explanation and prefer to have things "just so," then this idea of abandoning logic is going to feel very uncomfortable. However, if I may be so forward, I need to ask, *Has your faith in God dropped from your head to your heart?*

These are tough questions, I know. Don't shy away from them, and remember there is no condemnation for those who are in Christ. We proclaim our faith rests in the Lord, but many times when people struggle to let go of reason and logic, it is because their faith is still in their works. We need to shift from being dependent upon our efforts to be dependent on the Father's ability to perform miracles.

You need to have a good understanding of the difference between condemnation and conviction. Merriam-Webster's Dictionary defines condemnation as; *a statement or expression of very strong and definite criticism or disapproval.* It defines conviction as; *the act of convincing a person of error or of compelling the admission of a truth.*

The Devil wants to condemn you by persuading you to believe that God disapproves of you and sees you in a critical way. Whereas, the Holy Spirit wants to convince you of your error and compel you to walk in God's truth, as referenced in John 16:8 NLT, "And when he comes, he will convict the world of its sin, and of God's righteousness, and of the coming judgment."

Notice the heart behind each word and action. The spirit of condemnation is evil and seeks to force a separation—creating a feeling of guilt rooted in criticism. Convicting has a heart posture of correction and of wanting you to be convinced of God's righteousness. Notice also how condemnation is all about you and your wrongdoings, but conviction is primarily about God's character and plans. The Devil will always try to get your eyes off God and onto yourself.

Nothing about this journey is to bring condemnation upon you. Rebuke any condemnation in the name of Jesus! Romans 8:1 ESV: "There is therefore now no condemnation for those who are in Christ Jesus." 2 Corinthians 5:21 ESV: "For our sake he made him to be sin who knew no sin, so that in him we might become the righteousness of God." Declare this with me, "There is no condemnation for those who are in Christ. I am the righteousness of God in Christ!" Repeat this and meditate on it until your heart fully accepts the truth of God's Word. Then continue to meditate on it some more. Let it be a daily meditation so that you remain rooted in the truth of His grace and stay away from the traps of logic and reasoning.

EARTHLY IF-THEN VS. HEAVENLY IF-THEN RELATIONSHIPS

What better way to destroy a person than to whisper in their ear, "Let's be reasonable, you are not capable of much. Look at your track record." A small nudge in that direction and our internal dialog takes over. We begin reasoning with ourselves so the blow of failure won't hurt as severely, and the passing of our loved one won't be as devastating.

The trap is the reasoning itself. The seeds have been scattered, and now your reasoning is allowing them to take root. Meditating on the if-then has created a root for a problem that hasn't happened yet, and causes us to view our situation from an earthly, if-then perspective. You know, "better to expect the worst and hope for the best." I covered the deception of that statement in the first chapter.

Once those seeds are planted, the enemy's army can move onto the next victim. Given the proper amount of time to reason with ourselves, he knows we will self-destruct. Even if we don't fully self-destruct, Satan uses this tactic to delay our callings and to keep us walking by sight instead of by faith. During those times of reasoning, we become frozen in a circular pattern of thinking. We begin if-then-ing situations that do not have if-then relationships.

When we put our existence into perspective, we realize life does not neatly fit into if-then relationships. For example, if I add two plus two, then I will have four. That is an earthly if-then relationship rooted in unchanging facts. And for some comedic relief: if I go to college, then I will get a job in my chosen field of study. That is not an if-then relationship no matter how much we will it to be because it's not rooted in fact, but theory.

The problem is we are taught from a young age about these earthly if-then relationships which have no basis in the spiritual realm. Another example: statistics show that having a college degree will allow an average person to make more money throughout a lifetime than an average person without a college degree. That fact gets twisted into an if-then statement that looks like this: If I go to college, then I will be rich. We have a way of turning our theories, hopes, and fears into if-then statements that are not based upon facts. Sadly, we begin if-then-ing our entire life without asking God if our if-thens are even a part of His plan. We fail to acknowledge the if-thens rooted in His Word and how they function in the spiritual realm.

One reason we gravitate toward the if-then way of thinking is that it allows us to have a false sense of control. *If I'm married by twenty-three, then I can have my first home by twenty-five, and all my babies will be born by the time I'm thirty.* We end up believing that if we know how the equation works, we can plug in the numbers needed to create the outcome we desire.

Having a spirit of control can tow the same line as the spirit of pride. They both tend to be associated with abandonment and rejection. Many different spirits can manifest in a person from one single area of woundedness; for example, the spirit of control can be rooted in fear, rejection, abandonment, jealousy, pride, perfectionism, or independence. It can be different for each person. The outward expression of control can manifest in many forms and become rather difficult to detect because so many of the habits are not destructive but productive. What we gravitate toward during times of stress and overwhelm is a good indicator of where our heart is genuinely turning for comfort. Is your heart seeking to be comforted by the Holy Spirit, or is it seeking a false sense of control?

Maybe you know somebody who is continuously changing their hair color or style, and it seems to go along with different life circumstances. Do you know a chronic organizer who purges or reorganizes to the extent that they commonly repurchase items previously purged? Maybe you know someone who always buys a new car during significant life events. Some of the most dangerous expressions of a spirit of control are addiction, eating disorders, or an obsession with food and exercise.

Many young people have very little control over their environment and will form addictive habits. Some of these habits look very healthy. Their bodies and school studies are about the only two things they have any control over. Seeing extremes come about in either of those areas should be a red flag that there is a potential situation of overwhelm. How many of us have thought this one? *If I can control my surroundings, then nobody can hurt me again.* Not needing anybody, a spirit of independence quickly turns into a spirit of control once somebody does come into your life. They will have to play by your rules, or they're out.

I am not saying everyone who changes their hair, organizes, eats healthy, exercises, or is driven in their school studies, is dealing with a spirit of control. Having an orderly life takes self-control, which is a fruit of the spirit, and is an excellent thing to practice. Galatians 5:22-23 ESV: "But the fruit of the Spirit is love, joy, peace, patience, kindness, goodness, faithfulness, gentleness, self-control; against such things there is no law."

What I'm urging you to consider is where your habits gravitate during a crisis and high-stress times. What is the source of your motivation? Do you turn to Jesus during these times, or do you call your hairdresser? Do you seek Godly counsel from your friends and mentors, or do you find a new diet to start? Do you journal your prayers to the Lord, or do you get a new tattoo? The spirit of control can look very similar to a spirit of distraction. We begin distracting ourselves from our circumstances by pursuing control instead of seeking the Lord's will and comfort in the situation.

When operating under a spirit of control, we trap ourselves in the past and are unable to make decisions based on our hope for the future. You can't walk in the fullness of your future when trying to control it based on your past.

Here's my if-then for us today: if we want to live lives that don't leave us paralyzed trying to reason with the intangibles, then we need to learn the if-thens of the spiritual realm. Learn the if-thens created by God, not man! We need to understand the promises our Father created to govern our lives and use those as our guide, measuring stick, and planning manual. Here are some examples based on Jesus' Sermon on the Mount. It begins in Matthew, chapter five.

If I mourn, then I shall be comforted.
If I am meek, then I shall inherit the earth.
If I hunger and thirst for righteousness, then I shall be satisfied.
If I am merciful, then I shall receive mercy.
If I am persecuted and reviled for God's sake, then great is my reward in heaven.

Seek out the if-then statements of the Bible. Wash in the truth of spiritual if-thens so that the if-thens of this world don't become the meditation of your heart.

RESTING IN REDEMPTION

Rest. Doesn't that sound nice? But life is too busy to rest! We have deadlines, children's activities, dinner to cook, that thing called work, a house to clean, errands to run, volunteering to do for the school, church, and homeless shelter. Plus, we have family and friends to see, vacations to plan, parties to throw, animals to care for, cars to take in for maintenance. You want me to *rest*? Laughable!

Exhale.

OK. Please, hear me out.

How do you rest in redemption? According to Merriam Webster's Dictionary, one definition of the verb rest is: "to remain based or founded." Another definition is: "to cause to be firmly fixed." When you take these definitions of rest and plug them into the statement "rest in redemption," you get an entirely new perspective of rest.

"Remain based in redemption." "Remain founded in redemption." "Be firmly fixed in redemption." Wow! That sounds restful! Instead of leaning into your striving and leaning on things of this world, remain based, founded, and firmly fixed on His redemption. Rest in His redemption and finished work. Sound like anything you have ever heard before? "Seek thee first the Kingdom of God, and all these things will be added unto you." (Matthew 6:33 KJV) Focus on His redemption, and rest will overcome you.

When we choose to keep our eyes focused on Jesus' redemption and the completed work of the cross, we can't help but enter into rest. When we come to His feet with all our troubles and anxieties, we must pause our day-to-day activities, and, at that moment, we will enter into rest by default. Instead of trying to carry everything, we are saying to the Lord, "I give up. Help!" At His feet, everything moves from strife to rest. At His feet, you move from defeated to redeemed.

What does resting in redemption look like, practically speaking? The answer relies once again upon your motivation for the various activities in which you have chosen to partake. Resting in His redemption is not laziness or anything that looks like laziness. Resting in redemption means the Holy Spirit drives the reason behind your activity.

Yes, we all need to shower, clean our houses, put gas in our cars, and do the mundane day-to-day routines to function as contributing members of society. These are not the activities to which I refer. I am referring to the time spent on extracurricular activities. Why are you volunteering in four different places? Are you called to each one? They may all be good, but are they all of God? Why are your children stretched so thin between school, sports, church, music lessons, chores, volunteering, an after-school job, orthodontist appointments, social media, hobbies, and family and friend time? Are all these activities prosperous for their souls, or are they teetering with exhaustion as teenagers?

To rest in redemption, you must examine the fruit produced by every activity, commitment, and relationship. We must be willing to prune everything that isn't producing an abundant, Godly crop. I realize not every relationship that's lacking good fruit can, or should, be pruned off. However, we only have so much time at our disposal. Some relationships don't need to be pruned, but their watering schedule needs to be altered. Longer and longer stretches can happen between waterings, allowing other relationships to have more frequent waterings.

After examining some of your commitments, you may realize you need to step away and do some pruning in that area of your life. It doesn't mean it needs to be an ugly, rip-the-Band-Aid-off moment. Exiting any commitment should be done with grace and understanding for those who were dependent upon you. Don't leave people high and dry, but don't stick around for so long that you forget you were leaving in the first place. When we stay attentive to the Holy Spirit and self-prune, it is much more comfortable than when the pruning comes unexpectedly. It's the difference between trimming off the "sucker" branches or having to chop off an entire limb.

You must seek first the Kingdom. Seek first His redemption. Jesus says in Matthew 11:28, NIV, "'Come to me, all you who are weary and burdened, and I will give you rest.'" He will provide the grace you need to participate in the activities that will bear the most fruit. He will guide how to approach those various complicated relationships. Pruning certain relationships or distancing yourself with fewer waterings can be uncomfortable, but when done at the direction of the Holy Spirit, great peace awaits.

Don't think that since God called you into a particular area or relationship for a season that you must remain there for life. Seasons change, and so do the various involvements we have. One specific activity may have produced much fruit in your life and for the Kingdom, but when the Father calls you into a new season and a new direction, yield to His urging. It's in His movement that new limbs are grown and fresh fruit birthed.

When you engage in activities He has not called you to, you will strive and strive, exhausting yourself. As children of God, we have the promise that everything our hands touch will prosper. What happens when we choose to let the Spirit of God get behind our hands and direct the decisions? No longer is it a work of our flesh He blesses for our benefit, but it becomes a work of the Holy Spirit that blesses us and others for His glory!

Resting in redemption is when the switch in your soul goes from being earthly minded to Kingdom-minded. You no longer regard your time as your own, and you begin yearning to invest each moment you have into the things His Word says are important. You begin yielding your desires to the leading of the Holy Spirit, and once you do that, you have no option but to rest fully in His redemption.

The entire purpose in what Jesus did on the cross was to bring you from defeat into the fullness of His redemption. We need to be careful about what we believe about each season in our lives and how we label them. The meditation of your heart and mind will show what your trajectory is in the situation. I hope that you will choose the path that's aimed for the foot of the cross and rejoicing. That way, you can avoid walking in defeat.

It is time to get rid of all the earthly logic and if-then statements. Jesus' grace does not want to coexist with your works. His grace is sufficient and needs nothing added to it. Begin digging deeply, and search out the motivation behind your various habits. Whether they are productive habits or not, see what the Holy Spirit reveals. Don't be afraid of the pruning shears. Think of them like an exfoliation brush. They might lighten your load and smooth out some rough patches in the most joyous and unexpected ways.

Chapter 2: Primary Takeaway

- To get from defeat to redemption, you must discard all earthly logic and submit yourself before the foot of the cross and the promises of God.

Action Steps/Journaling Topics

- Does the idea of discarding earthly logic and reasoning scare you? Why or why not?
- Do you struggle with a spirit of control? What pain or fear triggered it?
- List the if-thens most often on your mind. Do they have a similar pattern?

- Have you ever mourned an event that had yet to happen or never happened at all?

- During the mourning of this anticipated event, did you notice your mind had shifted from focusing on God to focusing on logic? How did this affect your relationships?

- Learn God's promises and write if-then statements reflecting the truth of His Word. Look in the Gospels, Proverbs, and Psalms for inspiration.

CHAPTER 3

YESTERYEAR OR ANTIQUITY

CLEANING UP THE PAST

When we contemplate the past, it is intriguing to try and differentiate why specific memories fall into yesteryear, and other memories get relegated to antiquity. Merriam-Webster's Dictionary defines yesteryear as "time gone by: especially the recent past," and it defines antiquity as "the quality of being ancient." How is it that certain memories seem to disappear into antiquity, long forgotten, and yet memories that should have shifted to antiquity are still firmly planted in the recent past of yesteryear, brandishing great power to provoke us to tears and pain at a moment's notice?

The startling reality is that memories do not fall neatly on a timeline. Our lives follow a linear trajectory, but our memories don't play by the same rules. We all have our favorite family stories that we tell again and again. As time passes, those stories do not become less significant, nor does the joy and laughter they bring become diminished. What keeps those stories and memories secured in yesteryear? Why, after all these years, have those stories not been pushed into antiquity? The collection of happy memories has, undoubtedly, continued throughout my life and yours. Yet,

37

some of the freshest moments of joy seem to plunge into antiquity well before the appropriate time.

The same can be asked about our painful memories. Why do some wounds still feel fresh even after their yesteryear expiration date? The truth is, despite what you have heard, time does not heal all wounds. Time itself is not a mechanism for inner healing. We cannot apply the laws of our outer biological man to the laws of our inner being. Have you ever tried to force your memories into antiquity or resurrect others into yesteryear? It is an exercise in futility.

Our greatest joys and our deepest wounds do not play fairly with the rest of our memories. We unknowingly create a hierarchy with our memories where both the most joyous and most painful ones trump all the others for mental real estate. Prioritization is a natural occurrence, but we have to keep ourselves from erecting little monuments that become idols of false worship. We don't want to dwell with our pain, nor do we want to always talk about "the good ol' days" and rob ourselves of the hope of our future. The best is always yet to come!

QUICK REMINDER

In case you have already allowed some of the truth from the first chapter to slip into antiquity, let's review a few things. The painful memories are not something you deserve. The burden of pain from your past is not for you to carry, and there is no condemnation for those who are in Christ Jesus (Romans 8:1). Not all the painful memories we carry are transgressions by others against us. Sometimes the most painful memories are ones of our transgressions against others. We can easily allow our past failures to become a roadblock between us and the fullness of our future. Christ died for all your sins and the sins of those who have hurt you. Don't reserve any of God's wrath for yourself and don't walk in the defeat of condemnation.

Not all memories are created equal, and you should explore the ones that seem to linger. It is always easy to go on an adventure of discovery through our fields of joy. The sun is shining, the flowers are in bloom, and we exist as if we're in one never-ending exhale of pure relief.

However, trudging through the stench-ridden waters of our pain can be physically nauseating. Those torrential waters are, ironically, the very waters that help create in us a new character. Our thighs strengthen as we fight the muddy quicksand and get to solid ground. Once on solid ground, storms from above force us to army crawl, strengthening our core and our arms.

It's the army crawl to the foot of the cross that builds stamina and teaches us how to stabilize ourselves during any storm. After an intense workout, we always have to rest. You don't want to work the same muscles repeatedly. Otherwise, the exercises can become counterproductive, leading to weakness instead of strength.

Once we reach the foot of the cross, we must rest at His feet. After we have worked our muscles and taken a proper rest, we regain enough strength to stand and persevere—our endurance increases. We go from a place of defeat, grasping for the feet of Jesus, to the place of victory where we stand and raise our arms in worship of our Deliverer! Psalm 23:5 ESV: "You prepare a table before me in the presence of my enemies; you anoint my head with oil; my cup overflows."

We sit at the table He has prepared for us before our enemies. He will fight the battle if we will just get to His feet. Move when He says move, and go when He says go! He will provide the endurance you need to finish the race set before you. He will provide the stamina you need to trudge through the swamps of your past as you dig out the roots that have tried to entangle your legs. No more will the chains of the past be clamoring for your ankles! Hebrews 12:2 NLT: "We do this by keeping our eyes on Jesus, the champion who initiates and perfects our faith. Because of the joy awaiting him, he endured the cross, disregarding its shame. Now he is seated in the place of honor beside God's throne."

However, our reaction to the storm can create unequal strength within our bodies. We gain a false sense of endurance when we favor our strongest muscle group. Maybe your lower body powered you through the quicksand, but your upper body is lacking. Instead of transitioning to an army crawl once to the mainland, you continue to only push with your legs. Yes, you may make it far enough inland to be safe, but your face and body will have had to endure the mud, stickers, rocks, and twigs along the way. You arrive to safety only to discover more scars and pain than were necessary—scars and pain you could have avoided had you taken time to grow in strength and rest before fleeing the storm.

When we rely only on our strength, and our focus is on the end of the storm instead of the foot of the cross, we can miss some essential parts of the workout routine. We end up overworking a single muscle group and always skip the rest days. We create a false endurance based on our works instead of endurance rooted in the Spirit. Don't make the mistake of choosing work over waiting. You want genuine character, not a superficial counterpart. Sooner or later, the counterfeit muscles are always exposed because they can't handle the weight.

Can you identify with this analogy? Have you ever powered your way through a problem only to discover more pain and difficulties created along the way? Have you ever ascended to safety only to realize you were now squarely in the eye of the storm?

Ouch.

Me too.

Then again, maybe under the pressure of the storm, you have done the opposite. Is it possible the realization of your weakness caused you to freeze in the storm? Instead of building stamina and seeking safety at the foot of the cross, you decide it's too far to crawl. You have agreed to live in the middle of the wind and torment. You attempt to build yourself a makeshift tent in hopes of easing the pain of the hailstones. You live in denial that a storm is raging. However, as you lay there at night, you see the waters seeping in beneath your tent. You see the lightning flashes and hear the thunder roaring overhead.

You may have avoided the physical pain and scars brought onto those who powered through, but a different set of scars and wounds emerged: scars and deep wounds of fear. Constant noise will keep you from hearing the whisper of the Lord. A different set of memories and experiences is beginning to shape your path.

An unhealthy environment can do more damage internally than the hailstones you tried to avoid can do physically. Anytime we choose to rely on our strength, plans, and fortitude, we will endure unneeded pain. We will unintentionally spend much more time in the storm than we should have. Pushing through to safety or pitching a tent are inherently the same mistakes. They are practices in avoidance. Those habits keep your stamina and a completely mature character from developing.

The sooner we let the Lord become our trainer and follow His workout routine, the faster our stamina and character will develop, transferring the memories of pain to antiquity. A transfer that will free up spots in yesteryear for our joyous memories to stay firmly anchored and readily accessible.

The storms of life always present new circumstances so we can exercise new muscle groups. Making the army crawl to the foot of the cross looks different each time we do it. Making a crawl through the desert will have obstacles unique to the desert experience. Whereas, keeping your head above the rising waters of a hurricane is going to help you develop muscles you didn't even know you had when you were in the desert. The storms of life are fierce. They aren't pretty or fun, but when we see the destination is the foot of the cross, the place where He can give us rest, we don't care if our thighs are trembling under the load or that our brow is soaked with sweat because rest awaits. His redemption awaits.

Exodus 14:13 ESV: "And Moses said to the people, 'Fear not, stand firm, and see the salvation of the LORD, which he will work for you today. For the Egyptians whom you see today, you shall never see again.'" The storms of life may always present new circumstances, but He will do away with them just as He did away with the Egyptians, never to be seen again. We know that as we rest at His feet, He fights our battles and brings honor to those of us that humble ourselves before Him.

Exodus 14:14 NLT: "The LORD himself will fight for you. Just stay calm." I love the NLT version of Exodus 14:14 because it reminds us to remain calm. A workout can be intense, but it's nothing to panic over. We can stay calm through any storm because He is fighting for us. As we seek His wisdom, healing, and counsel, He lifts us from our army crawl to our place of triumphant rest.

The ability to rest, while exploring obstacles of our past hurts, is found in the truth of our identity. If you understand your identity rests solely in Christ, then you need not walk in defeat or condemnation.

Merriam-Webster's Dictionary defines identity as "sameness of essential character, the distinguishing character or personality of an individual, the condition of being the same with something described or asserted." The statement "My identity is in Christ" becomes "My essential character is in Christ," "My distinguishing character is in Christ," "My personality is in Christ." You gain a much better understanding of the scripture 1 John 4:17 NKJV, "Love has been perfected among us in this: that we may have boldness in the day of judgment; because as He is, so are we in this world." A scripture that allows us to boldly proclaim, "As Christ is so am I in this world."

You realize He creates the endurance and character in you that is pleasing to the Father and profitable for the Kingdom. You fully understand the most crucial part of your character, the thing that distinguishes you from the rest of this world, the root of your personality, is your identity in Him. No hurt or mistake from the past can overcome the name of Jesus. Your identity is in Christ. It's time to stop placing your identity in your strength, past pains, and mistakes. They were *never* meant to define you.

Forgiveness is a choice, not a feeling. Christ chose to come and die for us so that the Father would forgive our sins. When Jesus was in the garden of Gethsemane, He didn't much feel like going to the cross. He prayed three separate times that the cup be taken from Him. He was hoping there was another way, but there wasn't. He was willing to lay His feelings aside and yield to the will of God. He had to drink from that cup for the salvation of all humanity. For our forgiveness and right standing with God, Jesus had to choose something contrary to His feelings. He walked straight down the path leading to the greatest pain and anguish ever experienced by a human.

Maybe you are needing to drink from a cup which you don't much feel like drinking from. Sometimes forgiveness feels a little bit like a tortilla chip that you ate too quickly, and now it's going down your throat in a very uncomfortable way. Raise your hand, Tex-Mex fans; you know the struggle. Regardless, we don't always feel forgiveness. It's similar to how we don't always feel love, but we choose to show it. Does anyone have teenagers? OK, you get it.

Thank God we will never have to experience what Jesus experienced. However, that doesn't mean we won't face some complicated feelings and emotions when choosing to forgive. Some of you have gone through unimaginable things—situations that leave one speechless because the horror escapes words. Others might need to choose to forgive yourself for the things you have done either to yourself or to others. We have been freely forgiven and are called to freely forgive even when we don't feel like it. Colossians 3:13 NLT: "Make allowance for each other's faults, and forgive anyone who offends you. Remember, the Lord forgave you, so you must forgive others."

I have a bold statement to make.

Ready?

The sins committed against you were not committed by the person who hurt you, but by the sin living in that person.

Keeping this fact in mind makes it not only easier to forgive others, but also to forgive yourself. God calls us to forgiveness because it opens the door to inner healing. It's part of our identity in Christ. When our identity is rooted in Christ, He produces the character in us that can drink from the uncomfortable cup of forgiveness, thus allowing us to walk and be in closer oneness with Him.

Forgiveness is where a superficial character becomes exposed. The weight of forgiveness is very heavy if your muscles are counterfeit. However vast the cup of forgiveness might be, rest assured that as you lift it to your lips, it will feel light when the muscles you use are those developed from the endurance created by your dependence upon Jesus.

The uncomfortable feeling that comes when having to drink from the cup of forgiveness is oftentimes rooted in our desire for justice. The Bible says He will smite our enemies. And with a word like *smite,* you know we are thinking in the language of King James. Psalms 3:7 KJV, "Arise, O LORD; save me, O my God: for thou hast smitten all mine enemies upon the cheekbone; thou hast broken the teeth of the ungodly."

So, get to it, Lord!

Am I right?

That's how we can feel.

We were wronged, and now we need recompense. We need an apology before we can forgive. Or we feel we can never forgive ourselves and try to reserve some of God's wrath for ourselves. If this is you, then please reread chapter one. He forgave you. Now forgive yourself. But what do we do when we know we will never get an apology? How do we freely forgive yet turn to our Father to redeem and bring justice to the situation? What do we do when the people that hurt us are also Bible-believing Christians?

Forgiveness can only happen when you have a full understanding of how God's economy of redemption works. Remember, He brings blessings with no sorrow attached (Proverbs 10:22). He can redeem you while not needing to bring misfortune to you or the other party involved.

Yes, we all reap what we sow, Galatians 6:7 ESV: "Do not be deceived: God is not mocked, for whatever one sows, that will he also reap." However, as God's children, we are under the covering of His grace and need to maintain the posture that there is no condemnation for those who are in Christ.

We can't expect His judgement to reign down upon a fellow believer who wronged us when we know He wouldn't do that to us because our sins are forgiven past, present, and future. When we sin as children of God, we can open doors to the enemy, but God's wrath is not for us. As His children, we must never associate our sins with punishment from God.

Trials that seem to coincide with a sin we have identified in our lives are not from the Father but are instead an outward expression of the reaping and sowing world in which we live— reaping that the enemy will try to use to bring you under condemnation. The Father allows each trial to assist in the development of our character, but He doesn't pour out wrath upon us. His wrath poured upon Jesus on the cross. If God poured

His wrath upon us for sins already propitiated upon Jesus, then He would no longer be a just God.

We have to learn not to take the sins of other people personally. Every sin is rooted in the selfish desires of the flesh. The truth is that when people sin, they aren't thinking of you. The sin may directly affect you, but the real motivation is a personal outcome of the other person's desires. It may sound a little too *real*, but it is imperative to stop taking the transgressions of others so personally and instead seek to be compassionate.

It seems counterintuitive to seek to have compassion toward those who have wronged us, but asking the Father to give you a heart of compassion will allow you to cultivate a heart that naturally forgives and is rooted in patience.

Catch this: a compassionate heart is forgiving, patient, and filled with hope. Seek to be compassionate, and you will be able to forgive the transgressions of the past, be patient with the transgressions of the present, and be hopeful about seeing His mighty hand of redemption in the outcomes of transgressions committed against you in the future.

REMOVE AUTHORITY IN JESUS' NAME

Our memories stick around because we give them the authority to take up residence in our hearts and minds. We have mental real estate surveyed out and deeded specifically for memories.

I want to introduce you to the concept of your very own memory neighborhood—your memory-hood if you will. As we accumulate memories throughout our lives, we begin construction on our very own memory-hood. Each memory-hood has three phases of building. Phase one is our childhood; phase two, the adolescent years, and phase three is adulthood.

Many neighborhoods have Homeowners Associations (HOA) with varying degrees of restrictions. Homeowners must follow the restrictions to remain within the neighborhood. Their purpose is to keep the neighborhood looking and operating in a way deemed acceptable to all residents.

My question for you is how many of the homes in your memory-hood are currently in violation of your HOA's restrictions? How many doors do you need to go knock on and remind them of the memory-hood rules? The name of Jesus is on the deed for your mental real estate, and it's time everyone not in compliance gets evicted. They need their homeowner authority removed in Jesus' name!

When we look out from our balcony across our memory-hood to watch the sunrise, we are looking back toward the first phase of building. That first phase built during our childhood represents our earliest memories. Those formative years created many humble homes in our memory-hood. As our memory-hood expands, roads, sidewalks, and streetlights are all put into place. These provide ease of access and safety between our memories.

A common trait among the different phases of building in a neighborhood is that each phase consists of homes similar in size. The homes of your childhood should all be about the same size. Some exciting memories might have a second story. The wisdom passed down from a loved relative may not be an impressive home with a second story. Instead, those memories of wise words are a sprawling one-story home—a home that gives character to the entire first phase of the memory-hood.

The streetlights are brightly lit, the roads have no potholes, and there are plenty of sidewalks. You can skip from home to home as you reminisce on memory after memory. This is a healthy first phase of building. There is light, order, and peace. We all hope to look back toward the sunrise of our existence and see such order and quaintness. However, it's more likely that parts of our memory-hood need renovation or demolition.

I like to describe the memories that don't belong as high-rise buildings. Not because I don't like high-rise buildings. It's merely because a high-rise would not fit well within the culture or layout of a typical suburban neighborhood. You see, a high-rise is obtrusive—it obstructs your view. Its weight can cause cracks in the surrounding roads and sidewalks, and standard streetlights are unable to light it up properly. This allows a sense of darkness and uncertainty to lurk around it. High-rises also house a lot of living space for memories that are not willing to abide by the HOA restrictions. The mental real estate a high-rise requires can cause dysfunctions in the way you lay roads and sidewalks. A high-rise will keep you from skipping from one house of memory to the other because it blocks the view of other memories.

Keep tracking with me.

I want you to imagine you are looking from your memory-hood balcony, watching the sunrise. As you scan the horizon and see all the humble homes full of character and charm, do you see any high-rise buildings obstructing your view? Do you have any memories that have created a dark and uncertain area in your memory-hood, which you do your best to avoid? It's time to knock on that door with the eviction papers. Your mental real estate belongs to Jesus, and it's time to remind all those uninvited occupants they must vacate the premises.

What memories are you allowing in your memory-hood? Are you dwelling with pains from the past? We have all had those moments where we play a scenario over and over in our minds. We put it on repeat, trying to analyze each word said. Without fail, we come up with the perfect come back! But we'll never get to use that witty remark except in the replay in our minds.

Have you ever heard of meditation? Do you see where I am going with this? The more you allow yourself to meditate on your past pains and hurts, the taller that high-rise will rise.

Let's say a foundation was laid by the rejection you felt from your father as a young child. Then, while meditating on that rejection, story after story was built upon that foundation. The first floor is the floor of insecurity, followed by levels of sadness, anger, bitterness, perfectionism, and so on. The new stories accumulate as you meditate on the pain from the initial wound of rejection.

I know wounds hurt, and we go through pain in this life. I am by no means saying you should be an emotionless robot. Don't shove down your emotions and try to hide them. Feel the pain, cry, cry out to God, lament, but don't dwell there. Don't meditate on those pains over and over.

Immediately after we experience heartache, we can express our sadness before the Lord. There is a time for lamenting, but we must avoid allowing it to become what defines us. We need to turn our meditation to the truth found in God's Word.

The contractors that build these high-rises are never behind schedule. They are some of the quickest builders you'll ever encounter. They are erecting these buildings in the supernatural realm, and they don't have to get any building permits. Your meditations and thoughts give them all the building tools and permissions they require.

These builders are the angels that fell with Satan, and they can build on many foundations. One of their favorites is the foundation of condemnation. They can get a serious high-rise going on that foundation in no time. That's why we must let the Holy Spirit convict us to stop listening to the condemnation spewed by our adversary, the Devil.

2 Cor 10:3-5 NLT says, "We are human, but we don't wage war as humans do. We use God's mighty weapons, not worldly weapons, to knock down the strongholds of human reasoning and to destroy false arguments. We destroy every proud obstacle that keeps people from knowing God. We capture their rebellious thoughts and teach them to obey Christ."

We must understand that if we attempt to go up against these high-rises with human efforts, we will fail. No self-help book is going to tear that high-rise down because the answers are never within ourselves. Instead, we find solutions in Jesus, in the Word, and through prayer. Conviction and direction by the Holy Spirit will lead to the dismantling of a high-rise.

No equipment we have in the natural world is strong enough to tear down these high-rises once built. We can't buy a stick of dynamite and a bulldozer. Even if that were an option, we would end up destroying half our memory-hood in the process. The shrapnel from the high rise would burst through the windows of surrounding homes and infect even our happiest of memories.

The dismantling of high-rises must happen by taking authority away from the occupants and the builders, in Jesus' name. How exactly do we accomplish that? We change our meditations. We do as scripture indicates, and we take every thought captive to the truth of who we are in Jesus Christ. As we rest, forgive, heal, and take authority in Jesus' name, the Holy Spirit will begin dismantling the high-rises. He dismantles them in such a way that the process won't destroy even one blade of grass in the neighboring yards. You won't have to worry about any shrapnel or destruction, because destruction is not ever brought to us by the Holy Spirit.

The dismantling process will instead facilitate healing and restore your memory-hood to the peaceful place it should have been all along. The bad memories that should have been relegated to antiquity long ago will be sent on their way, allowing you the perfect view of your balcony sunrise once again, or maybe for the first time in your life. You will finally embrace the scripture about joy coming in the morning. Psalm 30:5 NLT: "For his anger lasts only a moment, but his favor lasts a lifetime! Weeping may last through the night, but joy comes with the morning."

AVOID BECOMING SPIRITUALLY STAGNANT

Hard right turn. There is nothing more refreshing than getting into the shower. Who doesn't enjoy the warm water and wonderful smells of shampoo and body wash? The water rushes over you and invigorates you for the busy day ahead. A hot shower helps you relax after a long day of work. It rinses away all the troubles and anxieties from the day, relaxes your muscles, and prepares you for a night of restorative sleep.

Well, have you ever been in a shower where the drain wasn't working correctly?

It's. The. Worst.

Instead of enjoying the refreshing warmth of the water, basking in the smells, and preparing our minds for the day ahead, we become occupied with the water collecting around our feet. We become rushed and agitated, enjoying our favorite scents is the last thing on our mind. Have you ever been in a shower where the drain is so clogged you have to shut off the water? Where you can only turn the water on long enough to rinse off?

This is a picture of spiritual stagnation. The refreshing waters of the Holy Spirit cannot flow in your life when you are standing in your waste. Instead of allowing the fresh waters to run over us and bring hope, our eyes shift to the dirt collecting at our feet.

Are you fixated on the water below you, or are you seeking to find out why the drain clogged in the first place? When we have too many high-rise buildings in our memory-hood, not only do we miss the sunrise and lose our fabulous view, but tall buildings are more likely to have plumbing issues. Dealing with our past isn't only so our memory-hood can be tidy, beautiful, and meet HOA standards. We must deal with our memory-hood to avoid becoming spiritually stagnant.

You can't be fixated on your past and expect to receive fresh revelation about your future. There's no room left for refreshing waters when your feet are still kicking around floaters from the past. Jeremiah 29:11 NLT: "'For I know the plans I have for you,' says the Lord. 'They are plans for good and not for disaster, to give you a future and a hope.'" It's time to rediscover the future He has planned for you. It's time to get the drain unclogged.

Shift your eyes from the anxiety-causing waste at your feet and enter into His refreshing waters where you can finally close your eyes and rest as He whispers His truths to your spirit. Isaiah 43:18-19 NIV: "Forget the former things; do not dwell on the past. See, I am doing a new thing! Now it springs up; do you not perceive it? I am making a way in the wilderness and streams in the wasteland."

It's time to reclaim your yesteryear memory-hood and send all those unfavorable memories packing into antiquity. Take a posture of rest before the Lord and stop trying to power through your circumstances on your strength. Likewise, it's also time to stop cohabitating with your pain. We are to rest and let the Lord fight our battles.

Through the process of being Spirit-led, we will develop the muscles and endurance the Father desires for us to have. His workouts always produce the best results. Get to the foot of the cross and let Him do the work. As you seek the Lord and ask Him to cultivate a compassionate heart in you, forgiveness and healing will begin to stir in your soul.

Remember, you must take authority in Jesus' name over all those uninvited tenants in your memory-hood. As a child of God and a coheir with Jesus, you have the power, in Jesus' name, to evict those noncompliant residents. Cleaning up our past is so important because we want to avoid becoming spiritually stagnant.

We need our drains clear and free from buildup because we don't want anything to impede the flow of Jesus' refreshing waters in our lives. His desire is for our cups to overflow, but He doesn't want them to end up drowning us. We should desire to be blessed so we can be a blessing, but that only happens when He doesn't have to restrict the flow of blessings in our lives because of clogged pipes. By cleaning up the past, our present becomes fertile ground for the Lord's overflow to bless others.

- We need to allow the Holy Spirit to direct the cleaning up of our past, so the refreshing waters of our future are not restricted.

Action Steps/Journaling Topics

- Do you have memories lingering in yesteryear that should have been relegated to antiquity long ago? List them.

- Of the memories listed above, do they stand so firmly in your mind because you tried to power through, and they left unneeded scars? Have you pitched a tent out of fear? Have you become so comfortable with the memories that you stopped walking the path to health?

- Why do you think you have chosen each action as it relates to your handling of the above memories? Why did you power through or pitch that tent?

- Are your feelings keeping you from forgiveness?

- In what areas can you begin cultivating a compassionate heart toward those who have wronged you? Have you allowed your trials to assist in your development of compassion toward others? How can your muscles of forgiveness go from counterfeit to secure in the Lord?

- When you look across your memory-hood, what authority have you granted to Satan's builders? Have your meditations given shape to any high-rise buildings that need to have their power removed? Is it time to evict the memories breaking the HOA rules?

- Are there areas in your life you feel have become stagnant? Is there a relationship between that stagnation and where your eyes are focused? Can you think of any drains needing cleaning for your refreshment?

- Ask a close friend for their observations and receive from them without ears of offense.

CHAPTER 4

PRESENT OR EXTANT

CLEANING UP THE PRESENT

Presently, the present is happening. Deep, I know. Pardon my fun, but the question is, *Is that enough?* Are we to be appeased simply because we are breathing? The question we need to ask ourselves is, *Are we extant?* According to Merriam Webster's Dictionary, the word extant is defined as "currently or actually existing, especially not lost or destroyed." As I read that definition, I begin to consider how many people are not *actually existing*. Am I *actually existing?*

Are we only *present* in our current relationships, or are we *extant* in our current relationships? Are we extant—actually existing—with God, or are we merely present with Him?

Nowadays, we have so many ways to be present. We have cell phones, email, social media, and video-calling capabilities on our devices. We have websites devoted entirely to posting videos for others to watch. We can be present in the lives of millions of people with a simple swipe of the screen. We have, unlike any other time in history, the ability to bring people into our presence at an unprecedented rate.

Are we treating our relationship with the Heavenly Father the same as the "relationships" we have on social media? Do we scroll and like His posts or post one for Him to see as we seek His approval? Do we go into His presence without *actually existing* there? Do we invite Him to our TED Talk without ever engaging and existing with Him? I don't like these questions either. They are zingers. Yet, I am having to examine these questions and hope you will join me.

I opened the introduction of this book with an expression of heartache over relationships reaching a point of improbable reconciliation. I struggled for many years with these particular relationships. I tried to keep myself present with the persons involved. Cards, phone calls, and gifts—all sent with hope. Hope that, if only they could see how much I care, they would also want to be present with me.

However, in the pursuit of being present, we can miss being extant. How do we know when to be present or extant? Should we pursue neither of them in certain relationships? Our society is programmed to be present. All the amazing avenues of communication can become burdensome. Social media, in particular, has caused numbers and presence to trump live relationships. Society has shifted from being extant in our relationships to struggling to relate on a meaningful level. Technology allows us to be present without having to reciprocate interest or involvement in other people's lives. We forget how to *exist* in a relationship.

Upon asking these hard questions, I had to look at my motivation for the continued effort to be present. I come from a family that was always very close. Aunts and uncles, cousins, grandparents, great-aunts and great-uncles, great-grandparents; we all did life together. We didn't have many friends because we spent all our time with our family. The initial motivation in seeking the presence of these people was because they are family. I sought their presence because it was what I had always known. I sought their presence because I still loved them even after being a casualty of their transgressions.

Raised to be a dutiful family member, I planned to make myself present for as long as it took. If only I could show them how much I care, then they would change and want to be present in my life.

A friend of mine from Bible study brought up a fascinating thought. Many of her stories and testimonies resonate with me. I see similarities in how we relate to people and how the Lord uses us to minister to others. We both have an affinity for sending cards and letters to people the Lord places upon our hearts.

While we were discussing sending cards and the like, she explained how the recipients of her cards or notes would thank her, and she doesn't even remember what she sent. To quote her: "I don't remember what I sent because it wasn't my idea to begin with." The revelation hit me like a ton of bricks. How many times have I sent a card or a letter and mulled over the fact that I received no response or reciprocation of affection? I have sent things and received responses running the gamut from no response to actual hate mail. I realize now, that at times, I was acting out of the flesh.

Those attempts to be present in someone's life were a grab by the flesh for a shiny object, not a leading of the Holy Spirit. Relationships, even unhealthy ones, can be very shiny objects. Maybe we should give more attention to that rusty trinket we left lying in the dirt. Please, understand I am not implying every letter or card must receive a reply to validate that it was Spirit led. I am, once again, urging each of us to examine our motivation. Let's dig into how we clean up our present and deal with some of the obstacles in today's relational atmosphere.

Everyone doesn't need to like you. To be universally liked by everybody is an impossibility. Jesus—God Himself in the flesh—was hated by a significant amount of people during His time here on this earth, and He was *perfect*.

Want to hear something shocking? You don't have to like everyone either.

Gasp!

How un-Christian of me to say such a thing. *Jesus calls us to love our neighbors, AJ!*

Well, guess what? Love has nothing to do with liking somebody. Whether we like them or not, we are to love them. And yet, we are also instructed to be very careful with whom we fellowship.

Fellowship means to be in company or companionship with others. Being mindful of our fellowship is of utmost priority. Healthy relationships reside on authenticity and transparency. However, when stuck in the world of people-pleasing, a wall gets built that keeps everyone at arm's length. When we try to people-please, we are operating under a spirit of the fear of man. This fear of man will keep us from being able to walk fully in the way the Lord has created us.

It's hard to be authentic when we are always second-guessing what others think of us. It can lead to a spirit of perfectionism. The adoption of that spirit into our personality will cause us to keep parts of ourselves hidden. I'm not saying every bit of us needs to be on display for all to see. We do need discernment from the Holy

Spirit about whom we allow into our intimate circle and what we share.

When you operate under a spirit of perfectionism and desire to be liked by everyone, you yield to the spirit that fears man instead of the Holy Spirit. When you are operating under a spirit of perfectionism and the fear of man, your ability to discern whom you should be in fellowship with is negatively affected. You begin to yield to the voice of your insecurities instead of the sound of the Holy Spirit. You may start working toward being liked by a person with whom the Lord doesn't desire for you to be in fellowship. People-pleasing leads to the facilitation of presence-based relationships instead of extant-based relationships.

We should desire that the Holy Spirit lead our relationships. Yes, we will have many acquaintances in this lifetime. There will be many friends, mentors, and work associates that will walk in and out of our lives. We are to love each of them, but we must allow the Holy Spirit to speak to us about with whom we spend our time. That same truth holds for family.

Please hear this: we are not obligated to be in a relationship with anybody, even family. Yes, we are called as Christians to the ministry of reconciliation, but again, reconciliation is a two-way street. Sometimes family members are the most toxic people you will ever encounter. It is an unfortunate reality, but a reality nonetheless. Likewise, when you see friends or family unrepentant of certain behaviors, you must remember that bad company corrupts good character. 1 Corinthians 15:33 NIV: "Do not be misled: 'Bad company corrupts good character.'" Family or not, you must allow the Holy Spirit to direct how much time you spend around specific individuals. The direction of the Holy Spirit might lead you to remove yourself from fellowship with them temporarily or entirely.

When you focus on people-pleasing and carry a spirit of the fear of man, then you will strive and strive to be present in a relationship. However, you will never be extant or actually existing in that relationship. A relationship can only fully exist when both parties involved engage for the proper reasons. Relationships based on your desire to be liked will always become one-sided relationships. There is the side where you will be the one putting in all the effort while being manipulated by the other party, or maybe your intentions were not pure in the first place, and you are seeking to manipulate the relationship.

Your people-pleasing could be rooted in trying to create favor with those you encounter. Favor only comes from the Lord. His grace supplies us with His unmerited favor. Consider Galatians 1:10 NLT: "Obviously, I'm not trying to win the approval of people, but of God. If pleasing people were my goal, I would not be Christ's servant."

A spirit to people-please will deceive you into thinking you can control and maintain the favor you receive. It's another example of when we allow the truth of God's grace to be replaced with works and striving. Striving for favor never works. Once you realize your people-pleasing didn't create the favor you were hoping for, you will bail on the relationship.

It seems rather innocent to seek to be liked. We all have that innate desire because no one seeks rejection. If you have noticed a pattern in your life of people-pleasing, you need to be aware that certain people will look to capitalize on your insecurities. We don't want to be taken advantage of, nor do we want to place people under an accusing microscope.

Seek the Holy Spirit's direction and yield to His voice. Don't yield to your insecurities. What kind of relationship are you cultivating if the motivation revolves around being liked or earning favor? It doesn't sound like the leading of the Holy Spirit. Spirits are leading that relationship and motivation, but not the kind of spirits you want leading.

Again, I implore you to examine your motivation and seek the Holy Spirit to reveal the root of your people-pleasing spirit. Is it rooted in a spirit of rejection, and you are trying to avoid pain? Or is it rooted in the Law, and you are trying to use works to gain favor? Maybe it has a different root altogether. If you tend toward the manipulative side of the above equation, then I would suggest you seek the Holy Spirit for deliverance. Seek a heart that desires to serve others instead of using others. Our hearts should rest in a desire to serve with no expectation of what we will receive in return.

TIME TO CUT TIES

Quick interjection: I am *not* speaking about marital relationships in this section on cutting ties. If you are in an abusive marriage, seek help immediately for both your safety and the safety of your children. If you are annoyed with your spouse or hurting and wanting to cut ties, then you need to seek Biblical counseling right away.

I had an inner turmoil over the realization that particular relationships in my life were going to have to be severed. It's what prompted the entire start of this book. I had hard questions I needed the Lord to answer. I needed the Holy Spirit to help me understand how to deal with and recover from hurts—past, present, and future. I needed to know how to reconcile the pains of life against His backdrop of redemption; how to continue to look forward with expectancy and hope for the future He has prepared for me. I needed Him to show me how to drain the stagnant waters of a broken heart from around my feet.

One lesson learned during this journey was that we could find liberation and freedom amid our sorrows. It sounds counterintuitive to say our sorrows thrust us into liberation and freedom, but at times we need to be shaken. When a situation shocks us, it allows scales of naivety to fall from our eyes. We seek fresh revelation. As we cry to the Father in grief, He allows the Holy Spirit to minister to us and bring truth and comfort to our hearts.

Had the events not taken place with the intensity and timing they occurred, then I would still be seeking the presence of the persons involved. I would still be subjecting myself to the bondage of unreciprocated love, stuck and shackled to the mirage of what the relationship could be. However, in God's grace, the sorrow shook me. As I grieved, the Holy Spirit gave me peace about cutting ties. It's incredible how, when our soul cries out in deep anguish, the Spirit of God can simultaneously provide comfort and peace. The peace and comfort we feel from the Spirit of God trickles over into our soul and brings rest to our weary hearts. This peace and contentment is another display of God's grace as we sort through the happenings of life and process the downloads from the Holy Spirit.

Cutting ties doesn't have to be permanent. We are called to the ministry of reconciliation as followers of Christ. To this day, if the persons involved in my situation were to seek reconciliation, I would embrace them. I have forgiven them and would be happy to reconcile, but I would also need to seek the Lord about how to proceed.

Reconciliation and forgiveness do not necessitate a reason to be extant in a relationship. We are not called to *exist* and do life with every person whom we have forgiven. In many instances, forgiveness is enough. Incorporating certain people into your life could be inappropriate and unproductive. Only the Holy Spirit can direct you when cutting ties. Sometimes the relationship was so one-sided that the other party might not notice your absence. Other times, you will find you are in an unhealthy relationship requiring a break-up of sorts. No matter the situation, the Holy Spirit will guide you and give you peace about how to proceed. The key is to obey His direction even if it feels uncomfortable.

A truth we need to embrace about life is that we only have a finite amount of time. We don't have an infinite amount of time here on earth. We need to make sure we understand that truth and how it relates to our relationships. The time we choose to dedicate to various people in our lives will mean we have less time for others. We have to learn to balance the time we have between daily living and the call of the Lord on our lives.

The truth is that you will never be able to spend enough time with your loved ones during this lifetime. That becomes painfully apparent when someone you love passes away. We always long for one more day, yet we can't spend each moment stuck to the hips of the ones we love. We all have different callings on our lives and separate paths the Lord has prepared. How do we rectify this dilemma?

We don't.

God, our Father, has already taken care of it. He promises eternity to those who believe in His Son. Each of those times we wished for one more day will not be in vain. We will have eternity with those of our friends and family who have believed in Jesus and accepted Him as their Savior.

What exactly does this have to do with cutting ties? The Father has already redeemed our time by giving us eternity. Cutting ties frees you from the unhealthy grip of unbalanced relationships. By creating distance physically and emotionally, it will allow compassion to grow in your heart toward that person. There might be some truth to the saying, "Absence makes the heart grow fonder." That heart of compassion will allow the Lord to use you as a powerful source of prayer for those individuals.

Cutting ties is not always an all-or-nothing kind of thing. As we seek to prioritize our time and become intentional in our relationships, we will realize that even some of our lifetime connections will not be able to take top priority in our lives. You can be extant in a relationship even when there is not frequent interaction. The determinants allowing a relationship to qualify as extant are transparency, authenticity, and genuine care between those involved.

There are those in our lives that no matter how long the happenings of life have separated us, once we get together—we never miss a beat. We sit with them, share our joys, worries, and hopes with no reserve. We encourage one another. We sit and truly exist with one another. Focus your energy on this type of relationship. We cannot afford to busy our calendars with relationships that never go beyond the surface level. Apply this to both your close-knit community and your corporate community. Seek the Lord as to how often you should engage in various relationships.

Breaking habits that promote presence-based relationships is a tricky directive to navigate. Breaking habits is something that exposes our hearts, sometimes in very uncomfortable ways, especially when a habit isn't inherently wrong or seems to be accepted by society as a whole. There appears to be a ripeness of excuses to argue the continuation of practices that aren't socially deemed wrong or, in some instances, deemed productive. The primary culprit promoting presence-based relationships today is social media.

Yep, we're going there. As a good friend of mine says, "Here. We. Go."

"I own a business, and it's all about being present for revenue."

"I'm a pastor and need to be present to impact the Kingdom."

"I'm in school and need to be present to feel accepted."

"I have so many friends and need to be present so that I can keep up with everybody."

Wow, none of those sound terrible. However, we need to examine our motivation behind wanting to be present in so many peoples' lives. Why do we want to be seen? Why do we want to know everybody else's business? Here's a good question: *What's wrong with being present?* The short answer—it's a waste of time in most cases.

We already covered how, in our lives, we have a finite amount of time. Let us not waste time on making ourselves present for vain pursuits or people-pleasing. No matter how noble we can make them sound, we must examine our motivations. Do hear me when I say this. Social media isn't inherently bad. No grave sin is committed because you have a social media account.

I understand that social media is useful for business marketing, keeping in touch with friends, ministering, and has many positive uses. I have a social media account and use it primarily for checking the news. I have lovely friends, who are very active on social media, and their humor blesses me often. So, why have I even brought this up?

The short of it: I want to shake you a bit.

Ruffle your feathers enough to see if you took offense to my statements. Ask questions that maybe make you uncomfortable enough to choose to examine your motivations for partaking in the social media realm. Don't allow condemnation to try and sneak in with my questions, but do welcome conviction if you need to make some adjustments to your usage of the various apps.

Unfortunately, the trajectory of our society has landed us squarely in the predicament of longing for community yet not knowing how to exist in the very thing for which we long. The answer has turned into making ourselves present, via social media, in the lives of others instead of actually existing with them. We make ourselves present to hundreds, thousands, or even millions of others and often neglect the very people with whom we have the opportunity to be extant.

Social media allows us to keep others updated about what's going on in our lives with no need to reciprocate interest in the lives of those who follow us. It's the perfect example of those one-sided relationships mentioned earlier and creates a dynamic that is rather unhealthy because there is no cultivation of fellowship.

Social media is a place where validation can be received without needing a genuine relationship with those validating us. A situation that can be very detrimental to those of us who already gravitate toward people-pleasing, because we don't know the character of the ones validating us. In the quest to become an influencer, could it be that you're the one being influenced?

In the past, relationships like the ones facilitated today through social media would have been considered a crime called stalking. What would we do if they changed "followers" to "stalkers"? Yikes! Would we still be so enamored with collecting as many as possible? I am using some extreme examples and comparisons, but I do it to jar your thinking. Are you missing out on life because of the device in your hand? Is time being taken away from important relationships where you need to be *extant*, in exchange for being *present* with others?

Reality TV primed us for the current relational atmosphere. Once social media was born, we could each become a reality TV star. The interest in amassing followers seemed to come with the promise of popularity and the end of loneliness. However, the shocking result has been the opposite. Instead of a world filled with more relationships than ever before, we have lost a significant understanding of how to exist in local community.

CHECK YOUR FOUNDATION AND REST IN HIS TIMING

There is no better time than the present to take a look at your foundation. Maybe some of the topics discussed so far have caused you to call in a foundation specialist for a checkup. Have you noticed some cracks in your walls? Is there tension in your foundation from shifting between works and the truth of grace? Hopefully, a curiosity about your motivations has sparked, and you are wondering if you need to be proactive before things get out of control, and your house starts to lean.

It's much easier to check for cracks in your foundation and have them repaired or put on watch than to wait until emergency measures are required to keep a disaster from happening. The easiest way to check your foundation is by sitting before the Lord in prayer and washing in His Word. Grab a coffee and relax. Be still before the Father. Pray for the Holy Spirit to answer the questions you have. Read Scripture and let it speak life and truth into you.

Do you believe the truths He speaks over you? Are you genuinely rooted in the security of His identity? Have you rejected the lies of the enemy and replaced them with the comfort and truth the Holy Spirit brings? Now is the time to dig into His truths so that when new trials come, your house will be built on a rock, not on sand. No longer will you seek to cover the cracks in your walls while trying to convince others you are "OK." Instead, you will let Him make the lasting repairs to your foundation, so you can take a rest from all the works you had to maintain. No longer will you be tempted to power through a storm or pitch a tent in fear. Instead, you will reach out, like Peter, to Jesus and ask Him to bring you out onto the water—no hiding in the boat, waiting for Him to calm the storm. You'll experience inner courage, given by Him, to step into the rough waters, knowing He is there to hold your hand. Where the Spirit of the Lord is, there is freedom (2 Corinthians 3:17). And no matter the size of the storm, if we stretch out our hand to Him, we will be safe, and we will be redeemed.

How is it that we are supposed to rest in His timing when it seems He didn't get the memos posted to my calendar?

The. Struggle. Is. Real.

I mean, we already covered the fact we *only* have so much time on this earth. *What's the delay, Lord? I'm not getting any younger!* But wait, I thought we just had a foundation check. How quickly we let the truth slip away. I know my Bible says He renews my youth. So, am I going to believe His truth, or believe the lie that I am running out of time? Lord, help our unbelief! And please help us to discover all the promises in your Word, so when lies come to deceive, we can respond, as Jesus did, with, "It is written…"

When we choose to rest in the Lord's timing, we don't have to strive. We can take our time, give our foundations a good looking-over, and repair areas that are allowing uninvited critters into our home. Resting in His timing keeps our eyes focused on seeking Him first, and on having a firm foundation. It keeps us from grabbing at our hopes and dreams before they are fully prepared for us. When we realize that God, the Creator of the universe, actually lives outside the confines of time, we gain a better perspective on His infinite patience. I don't know about you, but if I serve a God who isn't confined by time and space itself, then I am not going to question the timing He has prepared for my life. He can stop, freeze, and fast-forward it if He so desires. He can do anything He sees fit to accomplish the completion of His good works in my life and yours.

Let's rest in His timing and enjoy the foundation check because new trials will come to test that very foundation, allowing opportunities to grow our patience. At the same time, we wait for His hand to deliver us from our troubles. Romans 12:11-12 NIV: "Never be lacking in zeal, but keep your spiritual fervor, serving the Lord. Be joyful in hope, patient in affliction, faithful in prayer." Psalm 34:17 NIV, "The righteous cry out, and the LORD hears them; he delivers them from all their troubles."

There is no doubt that new trials will come while living in a fallen world, but we are always victorious because His shield stops every fiery arrow of the enemy. Ephesians 6:16 ESV: "In all circumstances take up the shield of faith, with which you can extinguish all the flaming darts of the evil one."

The hiccup is when we reach to pick up the arrow before it has had time to cool, and we get burned. That's what happens when you put new offenses, pains, or circumstances on repeat in your mind. You are creating a burn because you chose to reach out and touch something God has already defeated. Burns linger, and as you look at them each day during recovery, you are causing not only your mind but also your heart to meditate on the attack.

You are handing authority over to that circumstance to begin clearing mental real estate for it to spread out in any direction it pleases. Next thing you know, this new memory shows up with a bulldozer and destroys the cute memory-hood of happy memories and begins to erect a high-rise. Again! Amidst the destruction, the high-rise of pain becomes the single focus in your neighborhood of memories.

God intended to shield you and allow those hurtful accusations to fall to the ground as empty words. He intended to let that attack on your home, business, or character fall to the ground under the foot of His defeat. But instead. But instead. But instead, you picked the flaming arrow up and have now been burned. You surrendered your authority and forfeited the protection of His shield. We have all made this mistake at one point or another.

When you hand the authority of your memory-hood over to the high-rise–building scoundrels we discussed earlier (Satan and

72   THE GLASS DESK

his workers), then you will allow the entire culture of your memory-hood to shift. What once was a place of flower gardens, back-porch sunsets, and fireworks is no more. If the high rise is left to stand, say goodbye to your flower garden and sunsets. The sunlight is blotted out! No life can grow if the sun can't reach your garden, and no rest accomplished if you spend your entire day trying to navigate around the high rise trying to view the sunset.

By the time you get there, it's dark. You think maybe you can hurry back around to see the sunrise, but all you end up doing is chasing your tail in the darkness. Perhaps you're an optimist at heart and think, *Well, fireworks are beautiful in the dark!* I love your heart, and so does the Lord! However, a celebration will amount to little more than a slap in the face when you have a building blocking your view, and your neighbors are gone because their homes were bulldozed. There is no joy to be had in the memory-hood when you allow unwelcome company, at the forfeiture of your authority.

Time doesn't heal wounds, but Jesus does. Instead of handing authority to the scoundrel trying to rebuild the high rise, walk right to him and show the survey deeded to you. That deed has the signature of Jesus on it, and nobody has any right to come and bulldoze land belonging to you. In Jesus' name, you evict him from your memory-hood swiftly. Then, you call upon our Healer and Redeemer. When you call upon Jesus, the authority you have in Him goes on full display. With the return of authority comes an increase in territory. Your jurisdiction as coheirs with Christ entitles you to retake that stolen land.

The mistake we make is not stopping the high-rise builder immediately and instead choosing to meditate on that burn. Yes, maybe you took the bait, reached for the smoking arrow, and a few parts of your garden got bulldozed. It doesn't matter. Jesus can heal that burn in an instant and fix your garden with a breath—if you let Him.

However, if we don't let Him quickly handle the situation and try to care for the burn ourselves, we unknowingly hand over our authority. The meditation of our heart goes straight to building a high rise of pain and offense. It will soon become a towering structure that takes much more effort to demolish. When you meditate on the fresh, painful memories, you essentially become a subcontractor assisting the build, allowing the high rise to go up that much quicker. It's your memory-hood, and you need to assert your authority in Jesus' name quickly. Kick the builder out before he can even get a foundation laid, and seek Jesus for your healing.

CHAPTER SUMMARY

It's time to work toward extant relationships instead of presence-based relationships. Make a choice to be led by the Holy Spirit when deciding with whom to exist. Evaluate if you have a people-pleasing spirit, then seek the Lord to show you where it came from and how it developed.

Don't be afraid to cut ties with unhealthy relationships. Not everything profitable for our soul is necessarily comfortable. The persecuted Christian knows this truth all too well. The Lord will always profit our souls, but the road is rarely easy. Focus on breaking presence-based habits and reevaluate your social media use and motivations.

Check your foundation and have the ultimate builder shore up anything that seems to be out of place. Let Him patch the cracks as you spend your time learning the truths of His Word. Lastly, deal with new trials and offenses swiftly, so they do not become a foundation to a new high rise requiring precious time for careful demolition.

- Cleaning up the present can be uncomfortable, but in the end, when we focus on keeping a firm foundation of God's truth in our hearts, it will remove the temptation to reach out and get burned by those smoldering offenses.

Action Steps/Journaling Topics

- Write out the first ten relationships that come to your mind.
- Next to each relationship, give an honest evaluation of whether it is a relationship where you are present or extant. Are you actually existing in these relationships or just being present?
- Is each one of these relationships where you would like them to be? Some relationships will stay in the present-only category because that is where they belong, but do you see any that need to shift in one direction or the other?
- Are there any unhealthy relationships that need to have ties cut altogether?
- Does the thought of making relational changes cause you anxiety? Why? Could it be rooted in people-pleasing?
- How would you describe your social media habits? Are you happy with that description?
- How is your foundation looking? Do you feel that you are free of cracks, and no lies are seeping in, or do you need to be refreshed with the Word and meditate on His truths more than you have been? How could that be peacefully

implemented into your busy schedule and not done out of striving?

- Are you dealing with any new trials, or have you reached out and touched something that was still hot and caused a burn? Does social media cause you to reach out to touch those searing arrows shifting your meditation from His truths back to offenses?

- How can you cultivate a heart of compassion to help clean up new offenses and hurts swiftly?

CHAPTER 5

PROPHET FOR POSTERITY

UNFOLDING THE FUTURE

A year of planting! A year of growth! A year of reaping! In Christian circles, it is ubiquitous around the end of the year for us to begin praying about and discussing what word the Lord has placed upon our hearts for the New Year. In essence, we all become prophets trying to unfold our immediate future and that of future generations—our posterity. We seek fresh revelation from the Lord and boldly share our declarations with our other Christian-ese speaking friends.

I remember one year I felt as if the Lord said it was going to be *a big year,* and yet another time, He said, "It will be a year of change." The words were vague enough that, although I kept them tucked away in my heart as each of those years progressed, I had no idea what *big things* or *changes* were coming my way. However, I was excited and expectant to see the *big things* and *changes* that He promised would come.

Jump to December 2017 when my husband and I were wrapping up what had been one the hardest years of my life. Some pretty hard years have already disappeared to antiquity, but this one was still fresh. December has always been my favorite month of the year for many reasons—it's when we get to celebrate Jesus' birthday, it's the month I was born, it means a new year is around the corner, and it means I get to hear a fresh word from the Lord! His word for the coming year is always a booster shot to my hopes, and I can hardly wait for Him to reveal what He has planned! I was thirsty for new hope after 2017. I needed that booster shot as if my life depended on it.

The Lord didn't waste any time when I asked about 2018. His immediate response was, "It's going to be a bad year." You can imagine my surprise and complete sense of brokenness when the Lord allowed those words to enter my spirit. *What? NO! I rebuke thee, Satan!* (The King James is the only real way to rebuke the Devil, right?)

How often do we take things the Lord clearly says and assign it to Satan because we don't like it? (Singles? … OK, moving on.) I thought to myself, my Father wrote Jeremiah 29:11 NLT, "'For I know the plans I have for you,' says the Lord. 'They are plans for good and not for disaster, to give you a future and a hope.'" And did I ever need hope after 2017. My soul was devastated. I kept seeking the Lord well into the beginning of 2018, asking Him if I heard correctly, and it was confirmed—2018 was going to be a *bad year.*

What was I supposed to do with that? I usually share my word with everyone in my family and proclaim with joy how amazing the year ahead is going to be! Not this time. I was as tight-lipped about the coming year as was possible. I didn't even share it with my husband until all the *bad things* began happening. I remember finally confessing to my husband what the Lord had told me about the coming year. Seeing my husband's face and feeling the uncomfortable shift in his spirit flooded me with anxiety. We had already been through a year that we couldn't get away from fast

78   THE GLASS DESK

enough, only to receive a warning that the coming year was going to be bad as well. We didn't even get a warning for 2017, and it was horrific! How bad was *bad* going to be that it warranted a word of caution this time? You can imagine my distress.

I do want to quickly interject that our Father does not want us to have *bad* years, months, days, or moments. The Holy Spirit was not going to *create* a lousy year for me, but as the Father knows the beginning from the end, He warned of coming events. If your immediate thought was about a bad year you had, associating it with atonement for your shortcomings, then I urge you to go back and reread the first chapter of this book. Our Father will warn us of coming events so that we can prepare. Think Joseph in Egypt and the interpretation of Pharaoh's dream (Genesis 41). Moving on.

The Lord's warning was correct, and 2018 started with death, illness, lack, and the obliteration of the relationship I referenced in the introduction of this book. My family and I were not only experiencing these tragedies, but I was seeing them crash like a raging tsunami over the church body corporately. I eventually confessed what the Lord had told me to one other friend while we were having lunch early in the year. She shared with me that her boss was in the hospital, potentially on his deathbed, and requested my prayers.

My confession was not exactly what a fellow believer wanted to hear during a tough time, but I knew I needed to share what I had heard. She was the last person I shared the word with, leaving those "in the know" to just the three of us. Month after month passed, and I could see all the *bad things* unfolding before my eyes. I adhered to my Christian duty of searching for the best in each situation and would pray for God to use it to His glory, but even in those dutiful moments, my soul was wondering how long it could endure. I felt as if I was bursting at the seams and wanted to share the warning with others but never felt the Lord had given me His approval to do so.

As the year progressed, there was eventually a shift in the atmosphere. Around the end of spring and early summer, there were some heartbreaking moments, but there were also triumphs beginning to happen. Health restored, unimaginable provision poured out, and new relationships were being created. The Lord urged my heart to reconsider the word for the year.

The joyous events were beginning to take center stage, and the anxiety-inducing ones were seemingly losing steam. I started feeling as if the Lord was trying to get me to see it wasn't going to be a bad year. I just didn't understand why, if it wasn't going to be a bad year, had He even given me that word in the first place. He gave me the word and then I watched the *bad* happen month after month. I knew He had spoken. However, while watching the sad events, I never asked why it was going to be a bad year. Instead, I just accepted it and began to pray for those affected.

I can be slow at times, and I thank our Father constantly for His patience, but finally, one day, He blurted into my ear, "If you never faced difficult times, then why would you need me? Why would you need me if everything went perfectly in your life? What would I have to redeem for you if you never experienced loss?"

It jolted me, and I realized it wasn't going to be a bad year, but instead, it was going to be a year of redemption. The Holy Spirit highlighted the negative happenings with the word He initially gave to me. I heard *bad* year, and it became effortless to see the unfortunate events taking place. Since I never asked for any revelation about the word He had given, I just kept seeing the *bad* unfold.

Our Father in heaven *never* intended for us to experience pain or separation from Him. His desire was for us to be eternally joyful in His presence. However, He also knew we were going to choose otherwise, and, in His omniscience, He had a plan of redemption laid out from before the beginning of time. We are so blessed He had a plan to redeem our souls for eternity, and that alone is more than we deserve. To know He so loves us that He has used the riches of heaven to redeem our daily hurts and struggles is practically unfathomable! The depths of His grace and mercy can't be searched. Please allow those truths to penetrate deeply into your spirit.

After having the Holy Spirit reveal to me it was, in fact, a year of redemption, I was again hesitant to share the word because I wasn't sure if it was time to do so.

My husband had a truck for sale during this time, and as the middle of 2018 approached, it still hadn't sold. We already purchased a new truck for him the previous year and still had not been able to sell his old truck. She was a real beauty by any truck enthusiast's standards, and she was exceptionally good looking for being a work truck. We were a little impatient a few times with the truck not selling, but any time we have an item for sale, we always pray that whoever needs it the most would be able to purchase it. We rely on the Lord to bring the exact people He wants to bless.

We often joke that we make purchases to fix them up for the real owners God has in mind. Eventually, my husband received a call from a man in a town not far from ours, asking if he could come to see the truck during the approaching weekend. We were so thankful for the Lord's timing, but we were pretty firm on our price. Rather, *I* was pretty firm on our price and did not want to be haggled.

Saturday morning came. The man and his wife showed up to our home nice and early. We sensed a common bond as we engaged in introductions. After some conversing, we realized they were fellow believers and that the man was a pastor of a cowboy church located in his town. He had suffered an incredible accident in his last truck that should have taken his life. However, he emerged without so much as a cut. His truck, on the other hand, was totaled. Divine protection saved him that day.

After some wonderful and unexpected fellowship, the couple took the truck for a test drive and returned. While they were gone, my husband and I were discussing our minimum price. How much were we willing to negotiate on what we felt was already an outstanding deal? The Lord brought us a brother and sister.

He brought us the answer to our prayer.

He brought us the person who needed the truck the most.

He brought them that He might bless them.

How could we disregard that answered prayer over a few hundred dollars? We couldn't. So, when they returned, they purchased the truck and got the *deal* the Lord intended they have.

As they drove away, my husband and I had tears in our eyes. Nothing compares to those moments when God's faithfulness is put on such magnificent display. It was then that I felt led to tell my husband how the Lord redirected my heart about the word for the year. I shared with him how I felt it was a year of redemption instead of a bad year, as I had previously shared. I filled him in on how the Lord blurted some questions into my ears and got my attention about the matter. We chuckled over it while we rejoiced for the brother and sister who purchased the truck, and we walked back into the house.

At this point, even though I had finally shared the revelation with my husband, I had not spoken it to anybody else. I had it tucked away in my heart with expectancy. I was still operating under caution about sharing the new word because I had never experienced anything like starting with a negative prediction for the year, followed by a switch-up halfway through the year.

Two weeks after the man had purchased the truck, my husband received a text message from him. The man was reporting back just how amazing the truck was. He went on and on and then ended his text message with an oh-by-the-way-type comment. That oh-by-the-way was sharing what they decided to name the truck, and it was a message straight from the Spirit of God to my soul. They named the truck "Redemption."

I immediately burst into tears, as did my husband. At that moment, we breathed out the angst of the past eighteen months and breathed in the truth and promise of redemption. The Father knew the impact this display would have on our souls. He had been orchestrating it from before the beginning of time. Our Heavenly Father knew we were going to need reassurance more than anything in this particular season, and He had already choreographed the perfect dance between two families of believers navigating rough waters. Without the previous eighteen months of struggle and our brother's accident, this great epiphany would not have taken place in our lives. Our brother received a truck nicer than the one he totaled, and we received a direct word and confirmation from the Creator of the universe.

I was sharing the above story about the truck and how 2018 was a year of redemption with a couple we are close to, and upon finishing the story, I proceeded to tell them how the Lord didn't give me a word for 2019 in the traditional sense. Usually, I receive a word that creates an expectation of sorts: "big things," "changes." I can reflect by the end of the year on all the "changes" I saw, or all the "big things" that happened.

However, for 2019, I was given a directive. I shared with the couple that the Lord said, "Live." The husband of the couple said, "That sounds like rest." When he spoke those words, it was yet another eureka. Rest! For the first time in eighteen months, my soul was at rest, a peaceful rest. Jesus came to redeem us. Jesus came to redeem us so that we might have life and have it abundantly (John 10:10). God highlighted those hard moments we were going to face so that He could drive the truth of His Son's redemption deep into our hearts. He said to me, "Daughter, I have redeemed you. Now live! Take up your mat and walk!"

What on earth does this story have to do with being a prophet for ourselves or future generations? As I wrote the introduction to this book, I invited you to accompany me as I was to unfold my past, present, and future. I hoped that you would embrace, grow, and find meaning in your own story by hearing some of mine. How exactly do we unfold our future? How can we ever fully understand our story if it is continuing to be written moment by moment?

Redemption. Redemption is how you understand the unfinished story. Our stories were known beginning to end by our Creator before the beginning of creation. Did you catch that? Our Father knew all about our successes and failures—nights with tear-soaked pillows, and the days full of laughter before breath went into the lungs of Adam. He had a plan from before the beginning of time to redeem each one of those tears.

We have no idea what lies in the clutches of tomorrow, next week, next month, or next year. We can assume there will be joy, and there will be sadness. There will be good days, and there will be bad days. There will be forward progress, and there will be times of wandering, but the one constant is His redemption. The only thing we need to understand and unfold about our future is; despite what our future holds, He still chose to redeem it.

If we never experienced heartache and loss, challenging circumstances, or struggled with sin, then why would we need a Redeemer? What purpose was behind the shed blood and broken body of Jesus if not to redeem your entire story? He loves you. That is how you unfold your future. Spend your days meditating on the love and redemption of Christ. Do you know what will happen? What will happen is this: as you discover the height and depth of His love, you will become so rooted in the truth of His redemption that while seeking to unfold and discern your future, you have filled your present with a dynamic relationship of worship. Before you know it, your past has morphed into a solid foundation upon which your faith will continue to grow and flourish.

WORSHIP JESUS

That heading pretty much sums it up. Worship Jesus. As we seek to unfold our future, the most important thing we can do in that quest is to worship the one who came to redeem our future. The best is always yet to come. We only go from glory to glory. 2 Corinthians 3:18 NKJV: "But we all, with unveiled face, beholding as in a mirror the glory of the Lord, are being transformed into the same image from glory to glory, just as by the Spirit of the Lord." We are to live in hope as we seek answers about our future. Whether the Lord is speaking clearly, and we are in a season of rapid change, or He seems rather silent, allowing us to live in the moment, we need to be in a constant state of worship. We were created for His glory. When we dedicate our hearts and minds to learning His Word and choose to stand in praise of His greatness, we are doing more for our future than with any other activity.

The world says school, money, a spouse, children—those are the things needed to secure a prosperous future and legacy. It's a lie. A successful future lives upon a heart of worship. Our battles are fought in the spiritual realm by the armies of Heaven. In Psalm 68:25 NIV, who led the army into battle? "In front are the singers, after them the musicians; with them are the young women playing the timbrels." The worship leaders lead! This action was a show of the confidence they had in God. They knew, without doubt, He had already won the battle on their behalf.

We know our battle is won. Let's walk triumphantly with praise and worship on our lips as He fights for us. We need only be still and know that He is God (Psalm 46:10). Our future is, by default, full of battles because we have a loving Father who wants to give to us from the overflow of the storehouses of heaven, and that is in direct contention with this fallen world. This world seeks to discourage, delay, and destroy our hopes and blessings for the future. The battle will rage on, but we stand in victory when we stay grounded on His foundation and worship.

FOCUS ON THE PROPHETIC INSTEAD OF THE NATURAL

As we seek to unfold our future, we have two options. We can try to accomplish the task by looking at the events and realities of the natural world, or we can choose to focus on the promises of God and the prophetic nature of His promises. When we look at the natural circumstances around us, we begin to formulate a plan to improve upon those circumstances. That's what a successful future is, right? We each long to live in a better set of natural circumstances than our current positioning. Then, we pass that improved reality on to our posterity. None of us look around and say, "Things are going a little too well. I need to find a way to make my future less successful. How can I make a smaller legacy for myself?" Not. Going. To. Happen. I don't care who you are.

There is no inherent problem with making plans and setting goals. The problems arise when we base every decision on what we see in the natural instead of seeking the direction of the Holy Spirit. We can make plans, but the Lord orders our steps. Proverbs 16:9 ESV: "The heart of man plans his way, but the LORD establishes his steps." This part of unfolding our future very much relates to the previous discussion we had about earthly if-thens versus heavenly if-thens.

When we choose to focus on the prophetic, and the drains of the clogged shower have been cleaned, we can receive from the Lord without hindrance. No longer are we focused on the past floaters, or the present issue of too much water. Liberating us to a place of being able to close our eyes, enjoy the smells, and rest under His never-ending supply of refreshment. Focusing on the prophetic isn't about trying to control what He says or when He says it, but being an open vessel to receive when He speaks. The words of prophecy will pour into you through His Word, through your prayer time, and through your community. Frequently, you will hear and receive words of edification to share with those around you.

When our past and present are swept clean by His redemption, it frees us from bondage—turning our focus toward the Kingdom. I do want to caution you: living focused on the prophetic, and in a place of peace about your past and present, brings new territory you may not have expected, as it relates to relationships. The gift of living in the prophetic is not a gift every believer can receive. Notice I said not every believer can receive it. I did not say the Father doesn't offer it to each believer. The prophetic cannot be accepted by those who won't go beyond their past and can't take their eyes off the present.

When you begin to dwell in a place of prophecy, you will quickly notice those around you who are not capable of living in this type of existence. This dynamic can cause tension and eventually lead to reassessing with whom you can and cannot spend your time. Those who dwell in the past are miserable around those who live with expectant hope of the future.

REFLECT HIS REDEMPTION

Our futures should reflect His redemption. What exactly does that mean? Consider some of Merriam Webster's Dictionary definitions of reflect: "exhibit as an image, to make manifest or apparent, realize, consider." The definition of redemption is: "the act, process, or an instance of redeeming." The definition of redeeming is: "serving to offset or compensate for a defect." When we create new sentences using various definitions of reflect, redemption, and redeeming, the fundamental purpose of our futures becomes apparent.

My future should exhibit, as an image, His redemption.

My future should exhibit, as an image, His act and process of redeeming my life.

My future should exhibit, as an image, His serving to compensate for a defect in my life.

Our lives should be a living image of His power to redeem. The image we walk in should be one that consistently brings glory to His redemptive power in our lives.

My future should make manifest His redemption.

My future should make manifest His act and process of redeeming my life.

My future should make manifest His serving to compensate for a defect in my life.

Through our lives, we should be able to see the manifestation of His redemption. Each morning we are blessed to see His redeeming power. We have all fallen short of the glory of God, yet, Jesus has offset our defects. His redemption is made manifest in our lives most assuredly through His gift of salvation.

My future should make apparent His redemption.

My future should make apparent His act and process of redeeming my life.

My future should make apparent His serving to compensate for a defect in my life.

Once the gift of Jesus' salvation is made manifest in our lives, we should hope His gift of grace becomes apparent to others we encounter. As the Holy Spirit transforms us—sanctifies us into the likeness of Christ—our lives will have no option but to make apparent the power of the work He is doing within us.

My future should help me realize His redemption.

My future should help me realize His act and process of redeeming my life.

My future should help me realize His serving to compensate for a defect in my life.

When you come to the understanding that your future should help you personally realize His works in your life, your heart can't help but overflow with gratitude and love for our Father in heaven!

My future should cause others to consider His redemption.

My future should cause others to consider His act and process of redeeming their lives.

My future should cause others to consider His serving to compensate for a defect in their lives.

Once we realize the goodness and blessing He pours out, we allow our futures to reflect His redemption. The words of our testimony will cause others to consider these same truths—allowing His redemption to be reflected in their lives as the good news of the Gospel shines forth from us. The darkness of this world is so hungry to have something new to consider as they search for a way out of the darkness, and your life can be what causes them to consider Jesus.

As we seek to be prophets for our posterity and for unfolding our future, it is important to look at the image our life is projecting. Is His redemption being reflected through your life? Is the salvation of Jesus on display for others to see, and is the work of the Holy Spirit apparent? Worship didn't take up much room in the chapter, but it is so imperative to engage in daily worship before the throne of God. When we worship, the heavens open. Anytime we are in His presence, we transform. This transformation causes us to radiate the light of His glory to those around us.

Chapter 5: Primary Takeaway

- The Father has redeemed you through the blood of His Son so you might live, now! You don't need to wait for eternity. Your future lies in His redemption. As you meditate on that truth, He not only reveals your future, but he meets you in the present and transforms your past into a foundation built on the reality of His redemption. Live to reflect His redemption.

Action Steps/Journaling Topics

- What warnings have you received from the Lord? Share both past and present.

- Did you listen to or ignore the warning? And what were the results of your decision?

- Have you seen the redeeming hand of God move in your life? Recount some of those experiences.

- Does it excite you to think about unfolding your future? Or do you like to stay focused on the past and present?

What reasons are behind either choice and do you want to change at all?

- Do you spend time worshiping God each day? What does that look like for you? Praise and worship, art, dance? Have you had any desires to engage in new forms of worship?

- Which definition of "Reflect His Redemption" most resonates with you? Why?

CHAPTER 6

RENDEZVOUS FOR REVELATION

FINDING THE MISSING PIECES

Exceptional truth is hidden within the fellowship of believers because our Father created us for community. We never hear the church called the "church person." It's called the "church body" because it only operates in fullness when the children of God are in fellowship and service to one another.

I do hope throughout this book you noticed a pattern in the revelations I was receiving. They not only came from the Holy Spirit directly to me but also through revelation while in fellowship with other Christians.

From emails, text messages, and the physical lips of other believers, the Lord was able to bring my sense of revelation to an entirely new level. In so many instances, had I not been in fellowship, I would not have received the revelation in its fullness. There are many pieces to the puzzle of our existence, and our walk with the Lord.

Our salvation through Jesus, our deliverance, our quiet time with the Lord, the infilling of the Holy Spirit, our joys, and our heartaches are all pieces to the puzzle of God's plan for us.

However, I feel many believers are missing the most integral puzzle piece of all—community.

Picture the puzzle of your life this way. I know puzzles have become a thing of the past, but when trying to complete a puzzle as a child, we always searched for the pieces with flat edges first. It was much easier to get the border of our puzzle completed so we could better discern which remaining pieces went where.

A body has two hands and two feet. The people of the church are called to be the hands and feet of Jesus. Amid your life puzzle, there are two large handprints and footprints that you cannot fill. You can piece together your border and some inner pieces between the fingers or toes thanks to your salvation, the Holy Spirit, your passions, struggles, and triumphs. However, when looking at your puzzle, there will always be areas that are bare and lacking if you haven't filled those hand- and foot-shaped spaces with fellow believers and a church home.

Our Father never intended for us to be able to see the whole picture on our own because that's not how a family operates. Full revelation and a clear picture of your life can only come together while in communion with other believers. They have the pieces that are central to your puzzle! They are the pieces offering the most clarity while at the same time leaving the most substantial void if they are missing. It's time to find your missing pieces and get plugged into a community of fellow Bible-believing Christians.

"Wait one hot second! I have plenty of friends outside the church, and I don't need to go to church to be saved." Yes, indeed, your salvation does not rest upon your church attendance. Your salvation rests upon your confession as Jesus being your savior. His blood is all you need for salvation. This may be uncomfortable to hear, but when it comes to putting the puzzle of your life together to be viewed in Christ's fullness, any old friend with any old puzzle piece won't suffice.

Your puzzle pieces need to have a pattern of truth. A piece that only *almost* fits will just distort the design. Placing a different pattern at the center of your puzzle can confuse what you are seeing. The image you are reflecting through your puzzle (which should be the image of Christ) becomes blemished by the pieces that possess no truth. The impact of improperly placed puzzle pieces related to community has a far more reaching effect then you might realize.

Picture the borders of your puzzle; they hold everything in and build the foundation of your puzzle. That foundation is your salvation and the work of the Holy Spirit. You can have a completed border with a lot missing in the middle.

Then you have all the pieces that extend from the border to the center. These are your passions, successes, failures, heartaches, and the areas Christ has redeemed. His promises lace between the fingers and toes of the empty prints. Those missing handprints and footprints have the purpose of connecting more puzzle pieces than any of the other individual shapes combined. The width of a heel is significant to the size of your average puzzle.

I can hear you now, *But my puzzle is gigantic, and my friends have tiny feet. So, I can see most of my picture. I must be good ... right?* Nice try, but no. The two wide gaps created by the missing feet represent the church and corporate worship. The teaching of the Gospel to you while you also engage in corporate worship is paramount to your overall picture, and those two things alone will complete a significant portion of your puzzle.

The nitty-gritty comes when the handprints are both missing because those represent small groups and more personal, intimate fellowship with other believers. They represent the hands that pray with you, and that lay upon you for healing. They are the hands that serve you and lift you when you face challenging times. When these hand-shaped holes begin to fill, the promises of God suddenly become much more evident in your life. As the fingers stretch across your puzzle, a multitude of intricately laced promises can finally be connected. It's in these moments when our vision of the puzzle gains its most clarity and unity. The pattern becomes discernible when we fill those gaps with the hands of Christian fellowship. Revelation comes when we engage with our brothers and sisters in Christ.

Another interjection: don't turn seeking fellowship into a chore or duty. Pray and walk in faith that He will provide. Think quality over quantity. It is better to have a few trusted prayer warriors than a multitude of acquaintances. Hear me when I say this: church attendance and Christian fellowship has no relation to the status of your salvation. If you are not saved, you must first turn to Jesus and accept Him as your Lord and Savior.

Attending church and getting plugged into a small group is not going to complete the border of your puzzle and bring you salvation. Without the foundation and border of salvation, all your puzzle pieces are floating around with no structure. You will never be able to see the big picture of your life while stuck in that state.

You need to seek out the truth of His foundation before you worry about filling in the center of your puzzle. Also, this is not a call to avoid all non-Christians. We want souls saved, and we are called to ministry and the spreading of the Gospel. However, we should not use ministry as an excuse to associate with people and activities we know are inappropriate.

When you find yourself in fellowship with non-believers more than believers, you are going to start getting those inconsistent patterns in the middle of your picture, and they distort your image. Non-believers' lives do not operate under a yielding to the Holy Spirit and the wisdom of God. Instead, they operate under the logic of this world, and we know where that leads. It leads to a lack of revelation from the Holy Spirit in your life, and potentially some pretty ugly puzzle pieces intertwined at the very center of your picture.

A REVELATION ABOUT COMMUNITY

Ducks, chickens, geese, cats, dogs, donkeys, cattle, goats, horses, you name it—we either have some, or our neighbors do. As I mentioned before, my husband and I live in a little house, but I don't believe I specified we are also tucked away on a little piece of land where we have animals and a pretty nice view. It's a quiet place located in the prairies and small hills of north Texas where the wind bellows from one direction and then the next, all in short order of one another.

We have always wanted the Lord to use our home to His glory, and we pray over it often. We hope that when guests come to visit, they don't leave the same. We hope they will feel the presence of the Lord and have a sense of restoration upon departure. I was meditating on what we covered previously regarding the importance of Christian community. As I was sitting at my desk looking out across the fields, I began to ask the Father how we could use our property to facilitate opportunities for deeper fellowship within our church family—that is, outside the typical confines of four walls, a table, and chairs.

Immediately, He put into my spirit that we could use our property to help bridge the gap between the agricultural language in the Bible and our poor understanding of those principles in our modern society. As I was meditating on community, fellowship, and the references to agriculture in the Bible, my mind trailed off into thinking about all the exciting things we could plant.

As I was picturing all the beautiful plants we could bring home from the nursery, I had the thought that we wouldn't get the full effect of the reaping and sowing analogies because we would not be planting seeds. Instead, we would be planting growing plants, and some might already be bearing fruit. The Holy Spirit placed in my heart how this is an image of the Christian community and its importance for the growth of God's children.

You see, potted trees still need to be watered, pruned, and fertilized just like a tree planted into the ground. A potted tree will grow out of its current container and will need to be placed into a larger container to accommodate its maturity and the deepening of its roots. Large potted trees we find at nurseries have often had many different homes and traveled many miles of road throughout their lives. By the time we purchase them and plant them in their forever home, they have been nurtured by many different hands, all working toward the same goal of bringing healthy life to the tree—what a beautiful picture of how fellowship and community work.

As we walk out our faith alongside the Lord, He will bring various believers into our lives that will each water, prune, and fertilize us as we grow and prepare for our next season. There are many reasons people hesitate to get plugged into a local church or small group, but the truth is this: You can begin growing and even bearing fruit long before you are ever planted in your forever home. Some might even argue those years moving from pot to pot and traveling one road after another just might create the right atmosphere for some of your most fruitful seasons.

To allow the opportunity for growth, clarity, and abundance to pass because it's not your forever home would be such a shame. Get plugged in and start building those roots. When it's time for a new season, the Lord will have a fresh pot of fertile soil ready to take your roots even deeper.

As we fill in the missing pieces of our puzzle with community, our hearts will yearn more and more for that type of fellowship and edification. Thereby thrusting our roots deeper and allowing our canopy to become more sprawling and productive. The pieces will continue to be placed according to the Father's will, allowing His light to illuminate the revelation He seeks to reveal in us through the community in which He has placed us.

What a most fantastic picture of His desire to use relationships and community to connect the promises in your life! Isolation and superficial fellowship are the fast tracks to a wilderness season. It is impossible to grow stagnant in your walk with the Lord when other Holy Spirit-filled Christians surround you. It's through authentic, transparent fellowship that the Holy Spirit edifies and builds our faith in the Lord. We cannot reach the fullness God intends for our life alone, because their story is intertwined with ours as much as ours is with them. We all miss out on the fullness of our pictures when absent from one another.

Jesus is the Good Shepherd. Consider Matthew 18:12-13 ESV: "'What do you think? If a man has a hundred sheep, and one of them has gone astray, does he not leave the ninety-nine on the mountains and go in search of the one that went astray? And if he finds it, truly, I say to you, he rejoices over it more than over the ninety-nine that never went astray.'"

Jesus leaves the ninety-nine to find the one, but you notice His goal is always to bring us back into the flock. He desires to bring us back into community that is led by and gathered around Him. Yes, salvation is between you and Jesus. When we have gone astray, we are allowed to surrender to His goodness so He can guide us back into His flock. The choice to follow where He leads is left up to us. He knows community is where the fullness of the Christian walk lives, but He does not force it upon us.

COMMUNITY CHANGES

As resistant as we can be to change, sometimes the shift in our community atmosphere is a pivotal component to the calling God has on our lives. Remember, there are three types of people in your life—those there for a reason, a season, or a lifetime. Maybe you have a flat tire, and a good Samaritan stops to help you. You never see that person again, but the Father placed the Samaritan in your path to help you with a tire change.

An example of a person brought into your life for a season is the encouraging co-worker. You may not have a relationship away from work, but while employed together, your co-workers are very much a part of your daily life. As you face both hardships and joys, they will be there to encourage and celebrate alongside you. We all long for lifetime connections, but even lifetime connections can be seasonal and shift with the ebb and flow of life.

Some lifetime connections we are born into, and in healthy family relationships, those birth connections will last a lifetime. Some are made young, and other lifetime connections are made later in life. I have friends I know will be lifetime friends, and yet we don't have the opportunity to spend much time together during the current seasons in each of our lives—and that's OK. Seasons change, and so does community.

It's vitally important to have a close-knit community of fellow believers with whom you spend quality time fellowshipping. Iron sharpens iron, you know. However, outside of that close-knit group, you should see seasonal changes in those around you and within the broader corporate community in which you engage. This isn't a matter of seeking acquaintances. Instead, it is related to the evangelical work you are called to as a follower of Christ.

We covered the importance of choosing carefully with whom we spend time, but look to the example of Jesus. He had His "crew," so to speak, and spent the majority of His time with them. His iron was sharpening theirs, and today we have the Holy Spirit in each of us facilitating that same sharpening. However, have you ever noticed the community He actively engaged continually changed? Town to town and village to village He traveled seeking to bring the truth of the Kingdom of Heaven to all who were ready to receive. He had a world to impact and not a lot of time. Truth is this: our lives are but a small breath in the span of eternity, and we should seek to impact as many lives for the Kingdom as possible.

I am not saying we are all called to be traveling evangelists, but what I am saying is there should be refreshing waters flowing within your community. Stagnation in our community will undoubtedly lead to spiritual stagnation within our own lives. The Lord seeks to do new works and new things within our lives, and if we cling too tightly to the familiar and comfortable, our focus becomes the dirty water at our feet instead of the refreshing waters that come from the showerhead.

Instead of the drain remaining clogged by our past pains, we decide to cover the drain with our foot so we can enjoy the pleasant moments a little longer. The water is warm, there have been some great times, and we decide we would like to sit and take a bath. We cover the drain with our foot in an effort to savor the moments that have flowed into our life through the washing of the Holy Spirit. However, we will eventually encounter similar problems to when the drains were clogged. The water will have to be shut off to avoid drowning or causing a flood. We can create spiritual stagnation by limiting the flow of the Holy Spirit.

Many people are quick to forgive and heal from past hurts and instead get fixated on the successes and joys they experience. We should all allow our hearts to rest and meditate on the incredible blessings from the Lord. We should glorify His name with the words of our testimony, but we don't want our focus to become so stuck on blessings of the past that we avoid looking forward to our future. We all know what happens when we overstay our time in the bathtub.

What started with warm water, bubbles, a new book, a scent of relaxing lavender, and a cup of hot tea, quickly becomes something completely different. The water gets cold; the bubbles disappear, allowing you to see that the water has grown murky. The scent of lavender dissipates, you finish your tea, the book grows old, and your fingers prune.

Your soul will begin to grow restless and desire to turn on the water again, but until you remove your foot from the drain and let go of some of those enjoyable memories, the Holy Spirit can't begin to flow again freely.

Not only will community change, but so will your role within the community. As a follower of Jesus, you need to seek always to be sensitive to the leading of the Holy Spirit. There will be times when you are called to lead, times when you are called to support, and times when you will be called to rest. Maybe you have reached a season of leadership and enjoy it, so you decide to place your foot over the drain to control how long that season lasts. It may seem that works for a time, but once the tub hits maximum capacity, you have three options: you can remove your foot from the drain, turn off the water, or suffer the consequences of a flood.

If you remove your foot from the drain and allow the Holy Spirit to flow as the Lord sees fit, it could mean a shift in your positioning within the community. Remember, we only go from glory to glory! You may go from leading to supporting or resting, but the Holy Spirit will never mislead you. However, if you go with the other options, not only will you suffer the consequences, but the community will also develop a failure to thrive. We are called the body of Christ, and for a body to function properly, we need to yield to the placement the Holy Spirit desires for us within that body.

If you choose to turn the water off, you will see a decrease in anointing. The position you were called and anointed to have a portion of will be overcome with dryness, creating uneasiness and uncertainty, not only for you but for the other members of your community. Sometimes we place our foot over the drain once we reach a position we enjoy as an act motivated by fear. We like where we are and begin to fear that the Lord can do nothing more exciting and fulfilling than our current season. We thank the Lord for the blessing, cover the drain, and shut off the water. By doing this, we create unnecessary dryness. Instead of allowing the refreshing waters to flow in our new position and increase our anointing continually, we stop the flow, out of fear. Not only will we personally suffer, but so will the community.

Maybe you understand the irreplaceable importance of a fresh anointing and a flowing Holy Spirit, so you go with the third option and decide to suffer the consequences of a flood. You figure your cup can overflow and bless others. The problem with this thinking is that you are forcing your cup to overflow instead of letting it be a work of the Holy Spirit.

When the Lord causes our cup to overflow, He has storehouses prepared, and others lined up to be blessed by His outpouring on your life. On the other side of the coin, when you force your cup to overflow, there is no place for the waters of blessing to go. The timing is wrong. No storehouses are prepared, and no one has been ushered to you by the Lord to receive.

Instead, the tub overflows, and the rushing waters sweep the feet of those around out from under them. The community is hit first with a tidal wave of dirtied water that may, at first glance, seem to be flowing streams. Unfortunately, with no storehouse and direction for the waters, they end up soaking the ground and creating a stench of mildew. As the community members begin picking themselves up from the initial tidal wave, things may level out and seem to run smoothly for a while. The continual seepage of those waters may have lost some of their force and shock factor, but a community can only walk around in ankle-deep water for so long.

Eventually, they will grow tired of the murky water and the increasing stench of mold and stagnation. There will be an outcry for a cleaning crew, and this is when shifts within a community can become very uncomfortable. The body will only suffer for a short time before it seeks out a doctor, and the Holy Spirit is faithful to heal. We can easily avoid these situations of forced repositioning in a community if we will just keep our foot off the drain in the first place.

When I speak about shifting roles in community, I want to emphasize how those shifting roles are a shift in responsibility. As the members of our corporate community change, your responsibility in that community will go through seasons of change. What perceived responsibilities have you yoked around your neck? What responsibilities does the Lord want to take back from you or alleviate? Are there some yokes needing to be broken off because, although once they were easy, now they have become burdensome? The Lord will provide all the help you need in His perfect timing as you yield to His plan and the direction of the Holy Spirit.

COMMUNITY AND THE HOLY SPIRIT

Today I'm not sitting at my glass desk as I type this. I am currently in one of those yielded-to-the-Holy-Spirit moments I keep referencing. I happen to be sitting in a coffee shop in Minnesota, surrounded by the unfamiliar. I'm practically as far north as one can get on Interstate 35 and really can't give any reason for why I am here, other than that the Lord said, "Go." So, I went.

You see, my husband's line of work frequently takes him traveling, and although I always have joked about tagging along to his various destinations, not once, since 2010, when he started his business, have I accompanied him. I always stay home and continue with my typical day-to-day responsibilities.

What changed? There are a few things that changed for me to be where I am right now. One is our community, and two is the direction of the Holy Spirit. It's a straightforward concept—community and the Holy Spirit shape the trajectory of your life. Seek community to edify one another and illuminate revelation. The simplicity reflects the complexity of the work of the Lord in our lives. If we can just rest in the simplicity of His design, we will understand we need only seek Him, Godly community, and the leading of the Holy Spirit. Then He will take care of all the complex issues that so often busy us.

In 2018, my husband and I had a drastic shift in our community. We developed some very deep Kingdom friendships in a new, Holy Spirit-filled and yielded community that serves as an excellent source of encouragement and edification. I was ushered into a season of rest as we joined this community, and we have both had various yokes of responsibility broken from around our necks during this shift. Other yokes have been placed, but they are comfortable because the Lord has placed them.

My parents also moved to our neighborhood, and although they have always been a part of our community and we have deep relationships with them, the newfound proximity allowed a shift in our relationship to take place. It is a superficial change, but even when the shifts in our community seem very surface-based, they can still have drastic implications upon our day-to-day responsibilities and happenings.

If my parents did not currently live down the street from my husband and me, then I can most assuredly say the timing of this trip would not have allowed me to accompany him. The trip was very last minute, and with having farm animals, it takes planning to leave town. Never, have I ever been able to up and leave town at a moment's notice. That's the beauty of allowing the Lord to sort out the complexities of our lives. He knew all of this was coming, and with the move of my parents to our neighborhood, not only were many prayers answered, but it has set into motion an entire series of events that will continue to unfold day by day and year by year.

Community changes, and with that, sometimes the greatest blessings are simple ones—blessings of unexpected support lending peace to your day and helping to lighten the load of your responsibilities. Can I just ask you, right now, to allow the Holy Spirit to break off from you all the yokes of responsibility that don't belong to you anymore? Please take them off in Jesus' name.

The other change allowing me to be sitting in Minnesota at this very moment is the prompting of the Holy Spirit. The Holy Spirit is continually guiding and leading our lives, so that hasn't changed. What changed is the direction of this particular exhortation or persuasion. It's a brand-new work and leading. As I stated earlier, I have never, ever, accompanied my husband on one of his work trips. I have thought about tagging along at various times, but never felt led by the Holy Spirit to go and instead always yielded to the prompting to stay home.

Don't be afraid when the Holy Spirit prompts you to do something completely different than what you have been doing for the past ten, twenty, thirty, or more years. He has the complexities worked out and will provide all the help you need. Just obey in faith! When He says, "Go," … Go!

The tricky part can be when we become concerned with responsibilities or perceived responsibilities. Our flesh can want to shift back to those perceived responsibilities or obligations. We faithfully followed when prompted with a new and fresh direction, but then we begin using our experiences from the past to start dictating the course of the Holy Spirit's new work. When this happens we must pump the brakes and keep ourselves from tightening the yoke He is trying to loosen.

I have experienced this exact predicament and am so thankful for the fresh revelation the Lord provided. After being in

Minnesota for a total of ten days. My flesh began operating under its past experiences. I only ever leave home in ten- to fourteen-day increments when traveling. Therefore, I started looking at airfare to return home, although there was no prompting of the Holy Spirit to return home yet.

I began to reiterate to myself and the Lord all the responsibilities I have back at home. I was rather impressed with what seemed to be a list of urgent responsibilities, but I was getting no such feedback from the Holy Spirit. Each time I looked up airfare, anxiety would overcome me. What did I do? Simple. Stay until He says, "Go."

I encourage you to listen to those same promptings. The Lord will surround you with the community you need to feel at peace with His direction. Let the Holy Spirit use not only you in support of your community but your community in support of you.

COMMUNITY ISN'T PERFECT

Shocking! Isn't it? I talk all this talk about the importance of community and how vital it is to be surrounded by fellow believers. Then, BAM! I burst the bubble I just created for you. Life is so full of surprises.

The truth is this: community, much like church, will never be perfect because you and I are not perfect. Consider anybody you have ever lived close to—parents, siblings, college roommates, your spouse, or children—was it always perfect? Didn't at least one of those people get on your last nerve or hurt you? The answer is yes. Yes, you have been around people that annoy you, test your patience, and have hurt you both intentionally and unintentionally.

Don't get all holy roller on me now and try to act like all those annoyances and hurts didn't frustrate you at times. Remember this entire book, and study, is about being open and transparent with yourself. So, in the continued spirit of humility and transparency, let us choose to show grace to those in our community when they don't meet our expectations.

Let's also show ourselves grace when we don't meet our own expectations. Remember the freedom that exists when we have a heart well steeped in compassion. As our potted plants travel down the roads the Lord has planned for us, there will be some bumps and thorn bushes along the way. Don't let that make you grow weary of the journey. When you are on roads that feel lonely and desolate, remember, God was faithful to provide community before and is faithful to offer it again. Don't let the thorns on the neighboring rosebush leave you disenchanted. They, too, are a beautiful creation, and we need to allow the compassion developed in us to shine forth. The Holy Spirit will allow us to choose to see the beautiful flower instead of becoming obsessed with the potential threat of the thorns.

Another critical aspect of learning how to operate in community is to guard your heart against seeds of offense. When we walk in offense, we open all sorts of doors to the enemy. Offense quickly turns into bitterness, and we will no longer make decisions based upon the prompting of the Holy Spirit, but instead, make decisions based on logic and rooted in the flesh. The Holy Spirit gave you explicit instruction to serve in youth ministry, but *She offended me. I won't volunteer in youth again, Lord.*

You change course and decide to volunteer in Tech Arts so you can run the soundboard. You figure you are still serving, so everything will be fine. Right? You are now operating out of the flesh rather than the Spirit. God had encounters planned for you in youth ministry, and now, by becoming distracted with an offense, you will miss seeing and partaking of particular good works He had prepared for you. Remember, He works all for the good of those who love Him, and His purposes prevail, but there will be a loss of fullness when we choose to pull a Jonah. I encourage you to read the story of Jonah. We often think of it as a Sunday School story for children, but it is such a perfect example of some of the choices we make during our walk with the Lord. Jonah was a stubborn prophet, yet God still used Him. There is hope for us! We just don't need to make things any more difficult for ourselves. When God calls you to a particular community, don't run away. Stay, grow, and watch His miracles manifest.

Visit Mark 6:30-44 and read the story of Jesus feeding the five thousand. Notice Jesus called the disciples to go to a place of rest, but the masses followed. Jesus ministered to them, allowing the disciples to rest. Then as night approached, the disciples grew concerned about the people needing to leave and find food. Jesus wasn't worried and eventually told the crowd to sit in the green grass by groups of hundreds and of fifties. He blessed the bread, broke it, and five thousand men (not counting women and children) ate.

Twelve baskets of bread were collected from the five loaves. The thing I want you to catch from this story is how a miracle of multiplication took place in the context of resting within their community. When Jesus is in the midst of your community, and He is leading those you fellowship with, He will perform great miracles of multiplication in the lives of each person in that community. Not one person will go hungry, and in fact, there will be more than enough. The story says in verse forty-two, "and they all ate and were satisfied." Not one person was left hungry or wanting. That is the power of community!

Not a single person was forgotten, and there was a surplus on top of it all! I am so excited for you to begin experiencing the blessings of multiplication in your community. We may not be perfect, but we are ready for the miracles of the Lord. The fullness of God's glory is best realized in the ripples of community because His miracles get space to reverberate when we share our testimonies.

To find the missing pieces of our puzzle, we need to seek out and embrace Godly community. The Holy Spirit works in tandem with the community around us to bring to fullness the plans God has for our lives. We don't have to be in our forever church home for our roots to begin going deeper and deeper. Community will never be perfect, but He is, and we need to view our community through the heart of compassion He has cultivated in us.

Chapter 6: Primary Takeaway

- Community is an essential piece of your puzzle after having come to salvation. It will shift, it will change, and it won't be perfect, but it will be worth it. Be willing to let go of positions in your community so the anointing of the Holy Spirit will continually flow in you and through you.

Action Steps/Journaling Topics

- Have you ever witnessed the importance of community in your life? Tell me about the event.

- Are you currently plugged into a Christian community? If so, how do you feel about it? Are there deep, genuine relationships, or is it superficial?

- If you are not in community, are you searching for one? Why or why not?

- Do you feel you have chosen your community wisely, or do you need to reevaluate?

- Have you experienced a deepening of your roots in the Lord, even while not plugged into your forever church home? Have past communities watered, pruned, or fertilized you?

- Have you ever faced changes in your role in your community? Did you want to put your foot over the drain? Did you or didn't you, and what was the outcome?

- Have there been times when the Holy Spirit has prompted you to go in a completely different direction? Were you at peace letting your community step in and take over former responsibilities, or did you try to do it all yourself?

- Has the imperfect community around you hurt you? Are you willing to still be vulnerable with the Lord, allowing Him to guide you while in that community or usher you into a new community if He so chooses?

CHAPTER 7

THE UNEXPECTED BLESSING

PUTTING THE PIECES TOGETHER

His ways are not our ways. We hear that expression constantly and use it when we cannot explain the current heartache or trial a fellow believer is facing. We seek comfort in His ways being above ours. When we don't know the outcome, we rely solely on His faithfulness.

How often are we afforded the ability to see our heartaches repurposed into blessings? Or better asked as, how often do we take the time to look and see how the Lord repurposed our heartache? I am awestruck right now by the realization I am sitting at a desk completely compiled of heartache. I wept in gratitude over this desk the day the Lord had me assemble it, and my heart leaps each time I walk into my closet and see it! How can our hearts leap over something created from heartache? Allow me to explain.

At the start of this book, as I journeyed into writing, I explained how the catalyst was a newly fractured relationship, one I had held dear to my heart my entire life. The Lord encouraged me to write over the years, but the nudging fell on deaf ears and a weary spirit. *I'm not a writer; this idea to write is wholly ridiculous* and must not be from the Lord. He wouldn't set me up for utter failure and embarrassment. Who am I to think I could write a book?

These were the thoughts I often entertained, although I received encouragement from the most unlikely people and in response to the most unlikely of writings—you know, like emails. Can we just laugh out loud for a moment? Emails? Yes, I was always much more shocked than you are at this moment. I would giggle and then appreciate what a sweet soul a person must have to encourage my email writing.

I also received compliments from my professors for various papers submitted but always looked at it as a way for them to soften the blow that my technical writing skills were lacking. At least my research papers had something they found enjoyable—even if my sources were questionably cited. Is formatting *really* that important? It turns out it is, but that's neither here nor there.

The Lord always knows what's best, and He began having me pour my heart out while sitting in my bed one night. It was just me, my tears, and my laptop. As I started writing, the Holy Spirit began comforting me and bringing revelation and healing. The Father was redeeming my tears as they were falling. He sat with me as I cried out to Him in loss and heartache, turning the very words of my pain into one long-winded prayer written for all to see.

He showed me that through my writing, He could bring me to a new level of vulnerability and reliance upon Him. I have always been better at expressing myself through type rather than speech, and He had been waiting for me to obey. After realizing He had been right all these years (who'd have thought?), I began to long for a space to call my own. Space where I could sit and write, and not have to tuck everything back away each time I got up. You see, we live in a small home, and I love it, but I have never had my own space.

My husband always had his personal spaces, but *my* areas were public domain, if you know what I mean: the kitchen table, the coffee table, the bed—all spaces that I would sit, write and spread out. But then company would come over, or I'd have to deal with that pesky thing called dinner. Now all my notes were shoved back together, the books I had opened have been slammed closed and moved without a bookmark, and when I have something I must get written before I forget it, it can be a bit discouraging to not have my own space.

It only takes a few nights of your husband staring at you with concern because somehow, his side of the bed became your reference library while you sat there writing all day before you realize you need a new plan.

The desire to write had been growing with ever-increasing urgency, and I began to cry out to the Lord that if He was going to burden my heart with this desire, I needed Him to miraculously provide a space in our home. He showed me a spot in my closet right in front of a window that I could use. It was going to take a desk of just the right, tiny size, and I was going to be draped on each side with clothing—but it was going to be my space. I began looking online for desks that would fit. I checked every resale and wholesale website I could imagine. I found some contenders, but never once did I see a desk and think, *That's my desk!* I often thought, *This might do.* However, as you can imagine, *this might do* isn't exactly inspiring.

Through the years we have housed a few different young men the Lord brought our way, and having been in a pretty small house all these years, we have shuffled furniture from one room to another, many times. We also have various pieces of furniture sitting in our garage that we had purchased explicitly for said young men. Although I knew what furniture was in the garage—

none of which was a desk—I kept asking the Lord to show me my desk. You can see that I have fully rejected all logical thinking. I have learned that's the best way to see our Father perform a miracle. The Holy Spirit kept assuring me that I had what I needed, and I could not bring myself to purchase a desk.

One random, eighty-degree, Texas winter day, the sun was shining, and my husband told me I should get outside and try to enjoy some of the weather. I wholeheartedly agreed and planned to visit with my chickens, ducks, and geese out in their pasture and soak up some sunlight. Then, after getting dressed, the Lord put a strong urging in my spirit to go to the garage. I was excited! I knew there was a desk out there; I just didn't know where.

So, I did what any sane person would do—I went outside and stood in the garage with no plan. I kept asking the Lord to show me my desk in a garage that absolutely had no desk. After a bit of roaming in the garage, He brought my attention to a few different nightstands and shelving units, pointing out they could be the base of my desk. I took measurements and ran back and forth between my closet and the garage more than a few times.

Finally! I had the base of my desk—two silver wire shelving units that had three shelves and were very sturdy. Not only could they support a tabletop, but I would have space for storage as well. I also had the most adorable wicker baskets that fit perfectly on the two bottom shelves of the units. I could turn them sideways and use them to hold and display my frequently referenced books. I thought *Lord, you are on a roll!* but I still had no idea what was going to be the top of my desk. What on earth was in the garage that I could lay across these two units?

I carried those shelving units into the house in faith that, when I returned outside, the Lord was going to immediately show me what to place on those shelves to complete my desk. I figured I was going to have to use some of our two-by-four boards to construct a tabletop and was ready to go back outside and get the power tools. As I walked back into the garage, He immediately directed my eyes to an eight-foot-tall wardrobe we purchased for the first young man that came to live with us. It was black and had these excellent mirrored doors. I spoke out loud to the Lord, "Yeah, right!" as I laughed.

During all my meandering in the garage, I purposely never looked up to acknowledge this towering giant because it had become a bit of a sore spot. First, it was expensive to purchase and was going unused. Second, the parents of the young man we bought the wardrobe for treated us terribly and left deep wounds. Third, the wardrobe had been taking up a good portion of my garage for an even good-er portion of time.

However, although this wardrobe had been annoying me now for multiple years, and I had wanted to sell it multiple times, the Lord had never given me peace about selling it. Therefore, it stood and towered above everything in the garage and became the proverbial elephant in the room.

The Lord persisted, and so did I. He was performing a miracle that moments earlier, I was prepared to receive. I had abandoned all logic when He prompted me to go outside to the garage, but then He rubbed a sore spot, so I jumped onto the back of logic and rode that pony up to the Lord. I brought all my complaints. *Lord, you know I only have a two-by-four-foot space to put my desk, and that door is eight-feet tall! Plus, it's too heavy for me. How could I ever get it off the hinges?*

The Lord's reply was, "Go change your shoes." *What? That's all the response I get?* He was serious. I looked down at my flipflops and decided to heed His advice. My desk area is in my closet very close to where all my shoes are, and while I was changing my shoes, He showed me how to rearrange things better so that the desk *could* fit. I measured and re-measured, moved things here and there—it was going to work! That alone was a miracle. As I returned to the garage and approached the towering wardrobe, my only utterance was, "Keep me safe."

You see, not only is the door super heavy and tall, but the entire unit was sitting on furniture-moving castors, lifting the eight-foot structure an additional four inches into the air. As I type this, the Lord reminded me how, throughout the entire situation with the young man and his family, He kept me safe. All I had to do was follow His leading.

That day when I took the mirrored door off the wardrobe and brought it into this house, I struggled a lot, held my breath at times, exhausted myself—all while being delicate in my care of the door. The struggle with the mirrored door reflected the struggle with the young man and his family.

I made it into my closet.

He kept me safe.

He ignored my logic and performed His miracle!

I laid the door atop my shelves, and He introduced me to my very own space—the space He knew my heart would long for all those years ago.

I wept and wept. My heart was so full of joy, excitement, and gratitude. I could only exclaim, "Thank you! Thank you, Father! You inclined your ear to my heart. Thank you!"

You see, my heart began to ache after a yearning our Father placed within me. I could think of little else than my own space where I could sit and write. All along, He planned to repurpose my heartache and those sore spots into a blessing.

Sometimes we are so quick to want to purge bad memories and mementos from our lives, but maybe—just maybe—the Lord has plans to repurpose those hurts and those mementos into a blessing more special than we ever thought possible.

Now, every morning when I walk into my closet, the sun peeks through my window and reflects off my mirrored desk. My Glass Desk. *The Glass Desk*. My heart leaps with joy each time I see the space the Lord so faithfully supplied. He took that towering giant I had frustratingly hidden away in my garage, and He dismantled it. He cleaned it anew and moved it into my home, where it reflects His light, encourages me, and allows me to operate in the gifts He has given me. It has become my favorite part of the home.

I could have had any old brown, wooden desk. Instead, the Father provided me with a living space that is a constant reminder of His faithfulness and His plans to redeem every heartache I face. He has truly turned my sorrows into joy, and He wants to do the same for you. If we let Him, God will use the fragments of our heartache to build something entirely new—something full of life and His redemption.

During the writing of this book, the Lord restored our relationship with the young man and his parents. We were able to attend his wedding, and it just goes to show the redeeming and healing power of the Lord. We face trials, we face heartache, we don't always understand why things happen, but we grow. And we grow. And we lean upon Him. And we watch Him do new and unexpected works for His glory and His purpose.

Take notice of His redemption. It surrounds you daily if you will only look for it. Our hearts grow in peace and reverence for His glory when we meditate on His redeeming power in our lives. Meditating on His redemption is the crux to cultivating a heart of worship. As your mind replays all the blessings He has made manifest in your life and all the pain He has turned into joy, your heart will swell with gratitude and praise to the Almighty King.

Often, we miss the opportunity to take notice of His redemption. It can be easy to miss when you aren't looking for it. Frequently we take the posture of a blessing coming out of nowhere and never consider that maybe—just maybe—a particular blessing is an act of His redemption. Remember the time you spilled your coffee before ever taking a sip? Did you link that loss to the blessing of your friend treating you to a cup of coffee a few months later? Probably not. However, not only did He redeem the cup you spilled, but blessed you with company and good conversation on top of it.

We are hardwired to always look for the extravagant—the miracle. Today's cultural environment has created a mindset of consistently high expectations. Our lives have begun to neglect the small. The simple seems to no longer be worthy of appreciation. Still, if we shift our hearts back to focusing on the small daily redemptions of our Lord, then our hearts will stay primed and ready for worship. Allow the little things to be seen and felt as big things, and the big things to become even more prominent as you operate out of a place of enthusiastic praise.

Why does He redeem us? Why does it matter? Jesus redeems us for His glory and the glory of His Father, our Father in Heaven. The working of the Holy Spirit in our lives is to His glory and for our healing. Christ went to the cross to redeem us. He died so the veil separating us from God could be torn, and we could approach the throne of God as clean and spotless, covered in the blood of redemption.

The other side of Jesus going to the cross was the breaking of His body. By His stripes, we have been healed. His quest to redeem us was not only to save us from our sins and reunite us with the Father, but to allow us to walk in complete health—mental, physical, and emotional health. He took the abusive words, the hate, the beatings, and the torture so we could walk in fullness. His redemption completed. The Work finished. Let us posture our hearts to receive that truth and begin noticing the eternal redemption played out in our daily lives.

CHAPTER SUMMARY

Indeed, His ways are not our ways, and in the most confusing and irritating experiences we have during this life, He already has a plan of redemption. When we choose to let Him use people and things we don't really care for and fully surrender to His plan, our hearts cannot even fathom or contain the blessings He will create out of our heartache.

Just surrender. Give up control. Walk in faith. And let our Father perform His miracles. I can promise you won't regret it. It's OK to let heartache be a powerful motivator, because you know heartache will allow the beauty of His redemption to be on display in your life—a shining light of hope to a world so full of darkness.

May His light of redemption shine so brightly through your life that it draws all people unto Himself.

- The Father wants to redeem all your heartaches, and He is faithful to complete that work in your life. He has a plan, through the power of His redemption, to repurpose your sorrows into blessings. Just receive it!

Action Steps/Journaling Topics

- List the giants hiding in your garage. How long have they been there, and are you ready to let God dismantle them?

- Are you happy to ditch logic and let the miraculous reign, or do you scramble back to logic when you see the Lord using something or someone that rubs you the wrong way? List examples of the prominent pattern you display.

- What distractions are keeping you from taking notice of His redemption in your life?

- How can you position your heart to receive His redemption anew each day?

- How has this journey through your past and into your future changed your perspective?

- Do you view the puzzle pieces of heartache any differently now when considering the entirety of your image? What changed?

Next Steps

Make sure to stop by the blog at www.deskofredemption.com to read the most recent post and stay in the know about all the latest happenings.

AJ loves to hear and share stories of redemption. If you would like the opportunity to have your story of redemption shared in a future blog post or book, then send your story to stories@deskofredemption.com

You can visit www.redeemedimage.com to learn more about Redeemed Image's services.

Reviews are a great way to spread the word about *The Glass Desk*. Please leave a review and share your journey. Encourage others as they decide to take a seat at their very own desk of redemption.

ACKNOWLEDGEMENTS

Mom and Dad, it's finally finished! Both of you have waited so patiently, and I hope you enjoyed reading it.

Thank you, Kyle, for loving me even when my writing took over your side of the bed, interfered with your dinner, and our time together. Your patience and encouragement can never be replaced or overvalued. I love you so much.

Thank you to my family who encouraged me to keep writing. I have the most wonderful parents, grandparents, aunts, uncles, cousins, in-laws, nieces, nephews, and brother a girl could ask for.

Thank you to all my friends who contributed. You know who you are! Quotes, the title, pictures, and beyond, thank you for your love and friendship.

An exceptional thank you to the heartache prompting the start of this book. All praise to Jesus for He redeems!

AJ was born and raised in the great state of Texas, and she married the man of her dreams, Kyle, in 2009. It has been an adventure ever since. She calls him her business-owning, dirt-bike–riding, worship drummer. Shortly after they said, "I do," both of Kyle's parents became ill and passed away. Having gone from newlyweds to caretakers, AJ and Kyle navigated waters that most young married couples never face. These unfortunate circumstances thrust AJ deeper into her passion for nutrition and health, and her study in those subjects continues to this day. They have always joked that God sends them to boot-camp because He needs to train them up quickly for His assignments. They have spent almost their entire marriage in one type of ministry or another. Motocross ministry, death-row, and becoming legal guardians to teenage boys, all have had their challenges and rewards. AJ simply has a passion for reaching the lonely and broken-hearted. The desire to impact her community for the Kingdom led her to found Redeemed Image, a company where she uses her various giftings to the Lord's glory. They bought their first home way out in the prairies of North Texas and have been living the simple life ever since while becoming very familiar with dirt-bike tracks and farm animals.